God with Us

THEMES FROM MATTHEW

D.A. Carson

JKO Publishing, Inc.
Brentwood, Tennessee

Published by JKO Publishing, Inc.
7065 Moores Lane
Brentwood, Tennessee 37027
Printed in U.S.A.

Library of Congress Cataloging in Publication Data

Carson, D. A.
        God with us
        (A Bible commentary for laypersons)
        Bibliography: p.
        1. Bible. N.T. Matthew — Commentaries. I. Title
II. Series
BS2575.3.C37 1985   226'.207   85-10849
ISBN: 0-9645014-0-6

Contents

Dedication
To
Mr. and Mrs. R. T. Gemmell

Preface

Some people read the Bible the way a prospector looks at a mountain range; they do not really take in the spectacular panorama before them, but hunt around for odd gems. Gems there are in the Bible; but power, beauty, coherent argument, story, surprise, promise, moral instruction, and much more are also discovered by rapidly sweeping through a biblical book instead of lingering at each verse.

That is the sort of study this little book is meant to facilitate. It is not a detailed commentary on Matthew so much as an overview. Christians who want more help on details can profitably consult one of the commentaries mentioned at the end of this book.

May the God of all grace and truth be honored as men and women study His most holy Word and learn to live their lives in its light.

Soli Deo gloria.

D. A. Carson

Introduction

Strictly speaking, the Gospel we are about to study is anonymous. Nothing in the text itself tells us it was written by Matthew in the way that Romans 1:1 tells us the Epistle to the Romans was written by the apostle Paul. But early Christian writers are unanimous in seeing Matthew behind it, and there is no compelling reason to call their witness into question. *When* he wrote it is uncertain, though I suspect the date was about A.D. 63-65.

What is beyond all dispute is the fact that this Gospel enjoyed enormous popularity in the early church. Part of the reason is that Matthew records so much of Jesus' teachings—much more than Mark does, for instance. Not the least of these teachings are the five long discourses—Matthew 5—7; 10; 13; 18; 24—25—including the Sermon on the Mount.

But the book is more than a patchwork quilt of stories and discourses, loosely connected. There are themes that flow through its pages, connecting section after section. For instance, Matthew takes great pains to show how the birth, ministry, and death of Jesus the Messiah took place in fulfillment of the Scriptures. He is interested in demonstrating that Jesus is indeed the Son of David, the Son of God, the promised Messiah; but equally, he wants to make clear how most people's expectations of what the Messiah should be were woefully inadequate.

Occasionally it is possible to get a glimpse of the kind of Christian people to whom Matthew was writing. But we must never forget that this book does not set out to tell us about a church or an apostle, but about Jesus Christ. He is the climax of Old Testament expectations and the foundation for New Testament Christianity. Here in this Gospel is the dramatic *change* of covenant—when the old covenant gave way to the new, when the sacrifices of the Temple were replaced by the sacrifice of the cross, when the law of Moses was outstripped by the teaching of Jesus. Matthew's Gospel is the account of these fundamental changes. It tells us not only who Jesus was, why He came, and how He was related to the Old Testament Scriptures God had already provided, but also how the first disciples came to understanding and faith.

In short, the book we are about to study concerns Christian origins; and it is hard to imagine a Christian who is uninterested in such a theme. Moreover, because this Gospel ends with a commission (28:18-20), it refuses to be taken as a sourcebook for history buffs but no more. Rather, it lays the framework for Christian mission throughout the ages, and cries out to be studied and obeyed so that the purpose of Christ's coming may be accomplished in us.

If I were setting out to write an exciting and moving biography of a much-admired leader, it is very doubtful that I would begin by providing his genealogy. Such historical niceties, I might think, are often better restricted to an appendix printed in small type and tucked away at the end of the volume.

But Matthew didn't see it that way; and after reading his opening words—"A record of the geneaology of Jesus Christ the son of David, the son of Abraham"—his first readers wouldn't have either. For first-century, scripturally literate Jews, the proposal to set forth an account of the son of David would have to be authenticated. All it might promise of restored kingship (see 2 Sam. 7:12-16; Isa. 9:6,7), or of the son of Abraham, with all the rich allusions to the seed of Abraham who could usher in God's blessings not only on Israel but on the nations (Gen. 12:1-3), would have to be checked out. The prospect itself was wonderful, if true; but there were many imposters in the first century, men who claimed to be the Anointed One, the promised Messiah or Christ. One needed to be discerning. Jews who were interested in finding out more about Jesus, and Christian Jews who needed more instruction in the faith they professed, would have been eager to have before them the credentials of Jesus Christ.

Genealogy

Matthew took the opportunity to set forth more than a gene-alogical pedigree. He not only slipped in little asides, but struc-tured the list of names in order to make vital points. He thus transformed what might have been a dull recital into a thought-provoking introduction to his Gospel.

The first two-thirds of the names in this list can be found in the Septuagint (the Greek version of the Old Testament) of 1 Chronicles 2:1-15; 3:5-24 and Ruth 4:13-21. After Zerubbabel, Matthew relied on public records not found in the Old Testa-ment. Such detailed documentation was plentiful; Matthew would have found little difficulty in digging out the information. Interestingly, no twentieth-century Jew can prove he or she is a direct descendant of David, for the genealogical records have been destroyed by repeated holocausts.

When Christians compare this genealogy with the one pre-served in Luke 3:23-38, they notice that Luke went as far back as Adam, whereas Matthew went no further than Abraham. The reason is that Matthew was particularly interested in presenting Jesus as the fulfillment of many promises God made *to the Jews* as God's covenant people.

Readers may also puzzle over the fact that in Luke, Jesus' line runs from David though David's son Nathan (see Luke 3:31), but Matthew's record runs through David's son Solomon (see 2 Sam. 5:14). These and other differences are best explained in part by distinguishing a bloodline of descent from the succession to the throne. Luke traces the former, the actual line of Joseph; Matthew presents the latter, the way the line of David's *kingly* descendants ultimately found itself falling on Joseph. There are parallels in the British monarchy, when the throne succession jumps to another part of the family by default—as when there is an abdication or no heir.

Regardless of the details, both accounts pass through Joseph, even though he was not the real father of Jesus. There is independent evidence that Mary, too, was a descendant of David (see Luke 1:32); but the genealogies run through Joseph because the male line would legally establish Jesus' right to the throne.

Three notable features make this genealogy in Matthew stand out as a record that points to Jesus more than as a naked family tree. The *first* is the obvious division into three parts. The two crucial turning points that divide the genealogy make mention of David—*King* David, Matthew carefully points out (1:6)—and the onset of the Babylonian exile (Matt. 1:11,12) when the monarchy was destroyed and what was left of the nation was transported to Babylon in 587 B.C. From that time on, no heir of David sat on his throne. But now, Matthew was arguing, a descendant of David, Jesus Messiah, had come to take the royal reins in hand once more.

In fact, this fulfilled prophecy. The prophet Isaiah looked forward to a time when "a shoot will come up from the stump of Jesse [David's father]" (Isa. 11:1). That is, the tree representing the monarchy would be hacked down until only a stump remained, but from that apparently dead and ruined stump would spring a fresh "shoot" that would grow to become a solid tree.

In Stanley Park in Vancouver, near the entrance to the zoo, is just such a tree. A giant Douglas fir, ten feet or more in diameter, was cut down at shoulder height; but from the remaining stump the fir has sprouted a fresh tree, already three feet or so in diameter and growing nicely. In exactly the same way, the promises of God given to Abraham at the head of the genealogy issued in partial fulfillment in the middle third of the genealogy: King David and his heirs reigned. The Exile left only a stump; but now David's greater Son had emerged as the promised king from the same stalk.

Second, the breakdown of the genealogy into three series of fourteen is universally recognized to be partly artificial. Names have been left out. Between Joram and Uzziah (Matt. 1:8) came Ahaziah, Joash, and Amaziah (2 Kings 8:24; 1 Chron. 3:11; 2 Chron. 22:1,11; 24:27). There are other omissions as well. The expression translated "was the father of" often means "was the ancestor of" or "was the progenitor of;" and so the gaps are not themselves startling.

But the resulting neat divisions in the genealogy, besides

making the list easier to memorize, are probably meant to tell us something. Almost certainly the careful emphasis on the number 14 (Matt. 1:17) would prompt Jewish readers to remember that the numerical value of David's name in Hebrew was 14. (In Hebrew, each letter has a numerical value. Hence *dwd,* when $d = 4$ and $w = 6$, stands for $4 + 6 + 4$, which equals 14). In other words, this is a subtle way of emphasizing David's importance—and therefore the truth that Jesus is the promised Son of David. One of the three sets of fourteen is one generation short. Many suggestions have been put forward as to why this is so, none entirely convincing; and I do not yet know the answer myself.

The *third* and most intriguing feature of the genealogy is the mention of four women: Tamar (1:3), Rahab (1:5), Ruth (1:5), and Bathsheba ("Uriah's wife" 1:6). Most Jewish genealogies did not include women. More important, the choice of *these* particular women, instead of such great matriarchs as Sarah, Rebekah, and Leah, proves Matthew was giving us something more than merely biological information. Tamar seduced her father-in-law Judah into an incestuous relationship (see Gen. 38); Rahab saved the spies and joined the Israelites, but she was a pagan prostitute (see Josh. 2:5); Ruth was a Moabitess, not only a Gentile, but a member of a race frequently in bitter opposition to the Israelites; and Bathsheba who, though a Jewess, may well have been regarded by some as a Hittite because she married the Hittite Uriah. In any case she entered into the messianic line because of an adulterous affair with David (see 2 Sam. 11).

The kings and princes of this world proudly display their noble pedigrees, their links with dukes and duchesses, presidents and czars, prime ministers and tycoons. But Matthew took pains to point out that Jesus the King included in His heritage prostitutes and aliens. This speaks not only of His immense humility, but points to the fact that He came to "save his people from their sins" (Matt. 1:21), and to be the Lord and Saviour not only of Jews, but of men and women without racial distinction, fulfilling the promise to Abraham that in him all peoples on earth would be blessed (see Gen. 12:1-3).

Story

As compared with Luke's account of Jesus' birth, Matthew focused much more on Joseph's perspective than on Mary's. Following the customs of the day, Joseph and Mary became engaged to be married. Unlike modern engagements, however, theirs was legally binding and meant that they were regarded as husband and wife, even though they hadn't gone through the final marriage ceremony and begun to live together in a conjugal relationship. It was during this period of waiting that Mary's pregnancy was discovered, a pregnancy that had come about "through the Holy Spirit" (Matt. 1:18).

At that stage Joseph didn't know what we know from reading the first two chapters of Luke. In a society far more discreet than ours, it was unlikely Mary would have found either the opportunity or the courage to try to explain to him all that had happened to her. For his part, Joseph was in a terrible quandary. Because he was a righteous man, he couldn't bear the thought of going through with the marriage as if he had been involved in the illicit premarital sex that everyone would assume was the cause of the pregnancy. It would be demeaning and miserable; and besides, how could he ever trust Mary again?

But because he was also a kind man, he "did not want to expose her to public disgrace" (Matt. 1:19) by going through the common legal channels that could have granted him a divorce (as the breaking of an engagement was then called). Still less would he consider appealing to the capital punishment sanctioned by the Old Testament in such cases, but little if ever used at this time. Instead, he decided to use a legal loophole to bring about a quiet divorce that would free him from such a dishonorable marriage yet spare Mary from the worst of the shame.

At this point an angel of the Lord, appearing to him in a dream, changed his mind. Even the way the angel addressed him—"Joseph *son of David*"—would help prepare him for the astounding announcement (see 1:20). A moment's reflection shows how kind God was in securing Mary's permission before the pregnancy began, and Joseph's only after it was public. In any case, Joseph is here drawn into the mystery of the incarnation (literally, the "in-fleshing") and given the responsibility with Mary (see Luke 1:31) of naming the child Jesus. The name is the Greek equivalent of Joshua, which in its various forms means "Yahweh is salvation" or "Yahweh saves"—a name further eluci- dated by the explanation, "because he will *save* his people from their sins" (Matt. 1:21, italics added).

It says much for Joseph's faith that he went through with the wedding, regardless of what others might think; but even after taking Mary home as his wife (the high point in the final cere- mony), he had no sexual union with her until after Jesus was born (see v. 25).

Matthew tells us nothing of the manger or the shepherds, or even of the decree of Augustus Caesar that brought the couple to Bethlehem where the birth took place. Instead, he focused on another set of visitors, some wise men or "Magi" from the east (see 2:1-12; possibly they came from Babylon). The Bible does not tell us how many there were. The traditional three is a deduction in later tradition from their three gifts (v. 11). Appar- ently they were astrologers who mixed with their pagan super- stitions some knowledge of Old Testament promises of a coming Jewish king. The large Jewish population in Babylon may well have been the source of such information. Not knowing where to go when they reached Palestine, they headed for King Herod's palace to make their inquiries. Where else, after all, should a king be born but in the royal palace?

Little did they know that King Herod, now at the end of three and a half decades of rule, was a sick, paranoid, ruthless, and cruel man. Capable of competent administration and magnifi- cent building schemes, he had nevertheless become so petty and jealous of his position that he murdered his favorite wife and two of his sons when he feared that they might take his throne. The question of the Magi, therefore, was bound to upset him, and if Herod was upset so was Jerusalem (v. 3), for the people knew how vindictive their monarch could be. Even the religious leaders who were able to provide the right answer about the birthplace of the promised Messiah (vv. 3-6) were apparently more interested in placating Herod than in checking out the Magi's claims for themselves.

Traveling in the coolness of night was not uncommon at the time; and as the Magi set out again, this time for Bethlehem a mere five miles to the southwest, the star they had first seen in their own country reappeared. What kind of celestial phenomenon it was we do not know, although there have been many theories; but from their perspective, as they traveled, it hung over the town where the Child was. They soon found the exact house—perhaps by asking questions of the local people (see Luke 2:17,18)—and presented their gifts to the Child.

Despite the nativity scenes provided by modern department stores, the Magi did not join the shepherds around the manger. They arrived much later, by which time Joseph had managed to settle his family in a proper house. The two-year margin allowed by Herod (Matt. 2:16) suggests Jesus was at least a year old. The gifts themselves, gold and precious resins from rare trees, may have paid for some of the family's expenses as they undertook the lengthy trip and sojourn in Egypt. For that was what the Magi's visit precipitated: more angelic messages in dreams, a quick change of routes by the Magi, and an equally prompt departure by Joseph and his little family.

How many babies were killed by Herod's paranoid cruelty cannot be determined. Probably not more than a dozen were slaughtered, for Bethlehem was not a large village. But the anguish was no less profound for those who lost their young sons.

Not long after, Herod died. Joseph, instructed by another dream, returned to the land of Israel. But once more yet another dream was used to warn him away from Judea and Bethlehem; and so he went further north to his old hometown of Nazareth, and settled there.

Quite apart from the five remarkable quotations from the Old Testament found in these two chapters, the narrative itself makes some important points. Two stand out.

First, the birth of Jesus Messiah is presented as a stunning combination of the extraordinary, even the miraculous, along with the humble and plain, even the cruel and macabre. On the one hand, the conception itself owes everything to the supernatural intervention of God; and at every stage God's Son is protected by God's special initiative and direction. After all, guidance by angels appearing in dreams is rather rare in the New Testament—but it occurs five times in these two chapters! This Child was special, the fulfillment of Old Testament promises, the Saviour of His people, brought here with a divine commission. But on the other hand, He was born into a humble home and forced to flee His native land. His birth precipitated the savage murder of other young boys; and His parents were finally forced to settle in despised Galilee.

Second, there is an unmistakable contrast between the enthusiasm of the Gentile Magi and the reception afforded Jesus by His fellow Jews and by the half-Jewish monarch Herod. At best, the Jewish authorities were apathetic about the news, more concerned about political peace than determining the truthfulness of the claims the Magi made. The religious authorities had accurate scriptural knowledge, but no heart to seek out the kind of Messiah who was hidden in a village. By contrast the Magi came from a considerable distance and began their search from doubtful premises; but they found the Saviour, presented their gifts, and gave Him homage. Matthew, writing from his perspective after the cross and resurrection, perceived that the Magi worshiped better than they knew. They thus joined the Gentile women who made up part of Messiah's lineage, and anticipated the time when this Messiah would command His followers to make disciples of *every* nation (see 28:18-20).

Prophecy and Fulfillment

Perhaps the most striking feature of the birth of Jesus as presented by Matthew is the way each step fulfilled Old Testament Scripture. Five times the same point is made (1:22, 23; 2:5,6,15,17,18,23). Jesus was thereby linked with the revelation already given in the Scriptures before He was born—as surely as He was linked to the people of those Scriptures by the genealogy at the beginning of Matthew.

As we shall see, Christianity does not present itself as an entirely new religion, founded a mere two thousand years ago, but as the fulfillment of the revelation that the God of creation had already given, the climax to which God was shaping history.

That is part of the reason why Christians read the Old Testament along with the New Testament: the two parts belong together as components of *one* coherent revelation.

The nature of prophecy and fulfillment is often misunderstood. We sometimes think of it as nothing more than a combination of simple predictions, in sentences, followed by the dawning of the events those sentences predicted. In the Bible, that is *one* important kind of prophecy; but it is *only* one. The prophecy of Micah 5:2, quoted in Matthew 2:6, belongs to that kind. But there are other kinds of equal importance.

For instance, the Epistle to the Hebrews argues that the entire sacrificial system of the Old Testament had several built-in clues that made the entire system point forward to the greatest sacrifice of all—the sacrifice of the Lord Jesus Christ on the cross. Elsewhere in the New Testament, we learn how the law anticipated the gospel, how the levitical priesthood pointed to a new high priest who would effectively stand between God and humanity and never need replacing, how the ancient kingdom of David served as a model or "type" of the kingdom of God, how certain covenants had a built-in obsolescence that led believers to look forward to the dawning of the promised new covenant (Jer. 31:31-34) and much more.

The study of these kinds of prophecy is very important, for many of the links between the Old and New Testaments are of this nature. Sometimes the imagination of Bible students runs away with them, and they postulate very dubious links and play word-association games. For instance, some have seen in the scarlet cord Rahab tied in her window (Josh. 2:17-21) a strand in a long line of red or scarlet items that point to the blood of Jesus. But Rahab's scarlet cord is never used that way by later writers of Scripture, and certainly it is unconnected with any theme of sacrifice or atonement. A *scarlet* rope was probably used so that it would be easily seen by the invading Israelite soldiers.

The fact that many abuse this kind of biblical prophecy and make a rather silly game out of it, however, is no reason *not* to see its great importance. We should try to learn some of the controls that make it possible to handle such scriptural passages fairly and carefully. This is not the place to embark on such a study; but perhaps we can see how it operates in two or three of the fulfillment passages in these first two chapters of Matthew.

Consider the text quoted in Matthew 2:15. Joseph and Mary brought the toddler Jesus out of Egypt and returned to the land of Israel. This step, we are told, "fulfilled what the Lord had said through the prophet: 'Out of Egypt I called my Son.'" The passage quoted is Hosea 11:1. Close reading of that chapter, however, shows that the prophet in quoting the Lord's words was referring not to some *future* event but to a *past* event—namely, the time when God called His "son," the nation of Israel, out of Egypt at the time of the Exodus. So what gives Matthew the right to say that Jesus' exit from Egypt *fulfilled* the text in Hosea?

In fact, Jesus is often presented in the New Testament as the antitype of Israel; that is, the true and perfect Israel who does not fail. If Israel is likened to a vine that produces disgusting fruit (Isa. 5), Jesus is the true vine who brings forth good fruit (John 15). If Israel wandered in the wilderness 40 years and was frequently disobedient in the course of many trials and temptations, Jesus was sorely tempted in the wilderness for 40 days, but was perfectly obedient (Matt. 4:1-11). Israel in the Old Testament is the Lord's son (Exod. 4:22,23; Jer. 31:9); but Jesus, Himself a son of Israel, indeed a son of David, was supremely *the* Son of God; and therefore He re-enacted or recapitulated something of the history of the "son" (the nation of Israel) whose very existence pointed forward to Him.

Moreover, even in the context of Hosea 11, the prophet was looking forward to a saving invitation from the Lord (Hosea 11:10,11), thus falling into a broader Old Testament pattern that points in many ways to the ultimate self-disclosure of God in the person of His Son, the Lord Jesus Christ.

In a somewhat similar way, the weeping of the broken-hearted mothers of Bethlehem (Matt. 2:17,18) fulfilled the text from Jeremiah 31:15. That text pictures Rachel, the idealized mother of Israel, mourning because the nation was being transported into exile—the monarchy cut off and bloodshed everywhere. But Matthew, even by his presentation of the genealogy of Jesus, has shown that he understood the Exile to be coming to an end. True, some Jews straggled back to the Promised Land 70 years after the first transportations began, but the Davidic monarchy was never re-established.

With the birth of Jesus, that was to change. The shoot of David was coming to reign. The weeping of Bethlehem's mothers was to be the final stage of grief that belonged to the period of exile, and thus fulfilled it. As bitter as it was, it pointed ahead to the relief of the new covenant about to be inaugurated. Note that Jeremiah 31:15—Rachel weeping—is quickly followed by Jeremiah 31:31-34—the promise of a new covenant.

Perhaps the strangest fulfillment passage in these two chapters is found in Matthew 2:23, for in this case we cannot even find which Old Testament text is being cited! Of the many solutions that have been proposed, perhaps the simplest is this. Because for once Matthew does not refer to what was written by *the prophet* but by *the prophets* (plural), he is not referring to a specific text but to a theme found in many prophets—that Messiah would be despised (see Ps. 22:6-8,13; 69:8,20,21; Isa. 11:1; 49:7; 53:2,3,8; Dan. 9:26).

When the New Testament was first written, there were no quotation marks, so Matthew 2:23 could be translated, "So was fulfilled what was said through the prophets, that he would be called a Nazarene"—with "Nazarene" standing as a symbol for what was despised (see also John 1:46; 7:42,52). After the Resurrection, when unbelievers wanted to label the Christians in a sneering way, they referred to them as the *Nazarene* sect (see Acts 24:5)—and the expression was meant to sting, just as an Ivy League academic might sneeringly refer to a colleague trained in Podunk, Iowa or a prosperous sunbelt city might turn up its nose at Newark, New Jersey.

Jesus was brought to despised Galilee, to even more despised Nazareth, where He would grow up to win the label "Jesus the Nazarene"—not "Jesus the Bethlehemite," with all its rich Davidic overtones, but "Jesus the Nazarene." And this, too, was brought about by God's sovereign intervention, and fulfilled the Scriptures that predicted the Messiah would be despised.

But if Jesus fulfilled such Scriptures, He also fulfilled one that said He would be called Immanuel, which means "God with us" (Matt. 1:22,23). No greater blessing could God's people imagine than for God to be with them. Indeed, that will be the supreme source of joy in the new heaven and the new earth (see Rev. 21:3,22,23). God lives with His people! Already that joy and glory have manifest themselves in the one who is literally "God with us."

Questions for Further Study

1. What titles or names for Christ can you find in these two chapters? List them and explain what they mean.

2. Carefully compare Matthew 1:18—2:23 and Luke 1:2—2:40. How does each passage shed light on the other?

3. What implications can you draw from the fact that no modern Jew can prove he or she was a direct descendant of King David?

4. What implications for your own faith can you draw from the examples here of God's sovereign control of events to bring about His own saving purposes? (Read Rom. 8:28-39.)

5. What implications for your own faith can you draw from Jesus' willingness to humble Himself, to suffer rejection, and to be despised or ignored? (Read Matt. 10:24,25; John 15:18—16:4.)

6. What verses and themes in these two chapters already point to the cross?

The Beginning of Messiah's Ministry 2

Although the four canonical Gospels begin very differently from one another, it is remarkable that all four include some account of the ministry of John the Baptist before their descriptions of Jesus' ministry. The four evangelists rightly perceived that John's role as forerunner had been predicted by Scripture (see Isa. 40:3; Mal. 3:1; 4:5,6), and therefore they could scarcely leave him out. Indeed, including him helps to authenticate Jesus; for if Scripture says Messiah must have a forerunner, any messianic claimant must be able to say who his forerunner is.

But more important, Jesus' public ministry began from the time of His baptism *by John*; and so John's role demands some kind of attention. As we shall see in chapter 5 of this book, John's purpose in the unfolding of God's redemptive plan was carefully laid out by Jesus Himself, and was obviously a subject that interested Matthew.

The Forerunner
Most Jews believed that there had not been a prophet in Israel for four hundred years. The ministry of John the Baptist

was therefore bound to cause a sensation. Even the food he ate and the clothes he wore stamped him out not so much as poor but as a prophet, a prophet with obvious links to Elijah (see 2 Kings 1:8; Zech. 13:4). Matthew identified him as not merely a prophet (Matt. 11:9), but as the subject of one of Isaiah's prophecies (see 3:3)—an identification John the Baptist was prepared to make of himself (John 1:23).

But it was the burden of his message, and the spirit in which it was delivered, that commanded the greatest attention. As Matthew recorded it, that message embraced two crucial themes.

First, John announced the nearness of the kingdom of heaven (Matt 3:2)—the impending arrival of the Messiah who, unlike John himself, would baptize not with water but with the Holy Spirit and with fire (3:11,12). The word for kingdom might better be translated as reign. It primarily connotes the dynamic sense of rule, reign, or dominion rather than the relatively less frequent and static sense of territory or kingdom (as in 4:8).

This would call to mind for many Jews the numerous Old Testament promises of future blessing, promises sometimes couched in kingdom categories, and sometimes in other terms. There were promises to David's heir, promises of blessing and judgment on the Day of the Lord, promises of a new heaven and a new earth, of a regathered Israel and a new and transforming covenant (see 2 Sam. 7:13,14; Isa. 1:24-28; 9:6,7; 11:1-10; 64—66; Jer. 23:5,6; 31:31-34; Ezek. 37:24; Dan. 2:44; 7:13,14; Zeph. 3:14-20). All these and more are evoked by John's announcement.

But if the kingdom was about to dawn, there would have to be some mention of King Messiah. Here two things must be pointed out.

First, John the Baptist saw himself not merely as someone who gave a generalized prediction about some future kingdom, but as the immediate forerunner of someone coming after him whose sandals he was not fit to carry. That person would baptize the people with the Holy Spirit (for the messianic age would be characterized by the Holy Spirit) and with fire (here probably a symbol of purity, as in Isa. 1:25; Zech. 13:9; Mal. 3:2,3). But that same figure would effect a separation among human beings; some would be gathered like good grain and some, like chaff, would be destroyed (see Matt. 13:30). Messiah's coming, in other words, would bring both blessing and judgment, Holy Spirit purity and unequivocal condemnation.

Second, Matthew normally used the expression "the kingdom of heaven," whereas the other Gospel writers used "kingdom of God." The latter is used by Matthew in 12:28; 19:24; 21:31,43. It is very doubtful that the two expressions refer to different things. (Compare, for instance, Matt. 19:23,24 to Mark 10:23-25.) But the expression "kingdom of heaven" does have a certain ambiguity that Matthew may have preferred. Heaven, the place where God dwells, can stand for God, as in expressions such as "Heaven forbid!" It is a shade less specific, however. When we say, "the kingdom of God," we are referring to the kingdom in which *God* rules—even though the Gospel writers also made it clear that the kingship belonged, more specifically, to *Jesus* (see Luke 22:16,18,29,30).

But Matthew's expression "kingdom of heaven" left more room for this twin association of the kingdom to God and to Jesus. The kingdom truly is God's, and is doubtless assigned specifically to the Father (Matt. 26:29); yet it is also the kingdom of Jesus (see 16:28; 25:31,34,40; 27:42; possibly 5:35), for Jesus is King Messiah. Thus, when John the Baptist was preparing "the way of *the Lord*" (3:3), he was preparing, more specifically, the way of *Jesus,* since he was *Jesus'* forerunner.

The *second* feature of John's message was the call to repentance. Indeed, the urgency of this call to repentance was grounded on the nearness of the kingdom: "Repent, for the kingdom of heaven is near" (3:2). This was the way John the Baptist "prepared the way of the Lord." He demanded that men and women turn from their sins and get ready for the impending Messiah. Since His coming (as we have just seen) could mean either blessing or condemnation, it was important to get ready for Him.

Repentance is neither simply feeling sorry for one's sins, nor a merely intellectual change of mind about them. It is a radical change of direction, a transforming turn around of the entire person. It involves will and thought and emotion and action, and issues "fruit in keeping with repentance" (3:8). That is why John's language was so stern against the religious leaders of the day. The Pharisees and Sadducees were respected in many quarters; they were often devout and religious. But unless their lives demonstrated the radical transformation John was demanding, he treated them like other sinners.

More broadly, John the Baptist warned the people that reliance on heritage and racial and religious privilege would be of little use. Some Jews felt they were acceptable to God simply because they were descendants of Abraham and were therefore members of the covenant people of God. But John insisted God could raise up true children of Abraham from the stones of the ground. The argument thus laid the groundwork for Paul's view that the true children of Abraham are those who share his faith (see Rom. 4; Gal. 3).

The coming Messianic age would be so discriminating that any tree that would not bear fruit would be hacked down and burned. This view of the future was little appreciated by those who felt that just because they were Jews they would be all right, or that the coming of the Messiah would mean a great political transformation of Israel, freedom from the Roman overlords, and a restoration of Israel's earthly fortunes without any regard for the holiness of Messiah's people. But this Messiah, Matthew insisted, came to save His people *from their sins* (Matt. 1:21), not just from the Romans.

Connected with John's twofold message was his practice of baptizing those who confessed their sins. Baptism was not an unknown rite. For instance, some Jewish leaders baptized Gentile converts to Judaism; and some monastic Jewish sects practiced daily self-baptism as a rite of cleansing. But John connected baptism with repentance and the anticipation of the kingdom. So central a feature was this in John's ministry that it earned him the nickname "John the Baptizer," which we now abbreviate to "John the Baptist" (without any suggestion of denominational affiliation).

The Baptism of Jesus

But if baptism is linked with repentance, why did *Jesus* ask for baptism, since there was ample evidence that He never sinned and therefore had no sense of guilt and no need to repent?

John felt reluctant to baptize Jesus (3:14). Earlier he had rebuked the Pharisees and Sadducees because, unrepentant as they were, the candidates were not worthy of his baptism; but now he insisted his baptism was not worthy of the candidate.

It is doubtful that John the Baptist was quite clear that Jesus was the Messiah at this point; for according to John's Gospel, he did not recognize Jesus as the Messiah until *after* Jesus' baptism (see John 1:29-34). But there might easily have been another reason for John's reluctance to baptize Jesus. Even if he did not know Jesus well, it is inconceivable that his parents had never told him of the visit of his relative Mary, when both Jesus and John were still in the womb (see Luke 1:39-45). He probably also knew of Jesus' prodigious knowledge of Scripture, even as a youth (see Luke 2:41-52). The Baptist was a humble man. Conscious of his own sin and of Jesus' moral superiority, he thought it more fitting that he should be baptized by Jesus rather than the other way around.

However, Jesus' answer (Matt. 3:15) settled it for John. But His words "it is proper for us to do this to fulfill all righteousness" are not easy to understand. Some have argued, for instance, that by His baptism Jesus was anticipating His "baptism of death" by which He would secure righteousness for many. But the text speaks of *both* Jesus *and* John involved in an action that fulfills all righteousness, so it cannot refer to a *shared* death; and in this Gospel, righteousness is not used to refer to what Christ by His death secured for others, but to life and conduct that conform to God's will.

It seems best therefore to understand Jesus' argument another way. John's baptism was tied with *both* roles of His ministry; it was connected both with repentance and with the announcement of the kingdom. Jesus was saying that for Him to be baptized by the Baptist would be proper for *both* participants, because it would fulfill all righteousness. That is, it would point to the complete righteousness of those who do the Father's will. Even in the Old Testament, a chief characteristic of the Suffering Servant was obedience to the will of God; for the Servant suffered and died to accomplish redemption in obedience to the will of God. Since John's baptism pointed to the Messianic age, Jesus' submission to that baptism became a way of affirming His determination to accomplish His assigned work.

And so Jesus was baptized. The rightness of the step was affirmed by the vision of the Spirit descending upon Him like a dove and the testimony of the voice from heaven saying, "This is my Son, whom I love; with him I am well pleased" (3:17). These words combine fragments from two Old Testament texts— Isaiah 42:1 and Psalm 2:7. Together they make several important points. Jesus is pointed out to be the true and beloved Son of God and the obedient Suffering Servant predicted by Isaiah. The Spirit rested on Jesus (fulfilling Isa. 42:1-4) not to change Jesus' status or to assign Him certain rights, but to identify Him as the promised Servant and Son, the Messiah whose kingdom John the Baptist had been announcing, and to announce the beginning of His public ministry.

The Temptation of Jesus

One might have expected Jesus to move directly from such a dramatic display of the Father's pleasure to powerful public ministry, but that was not God's way. The first thing the Spirit who had come to rest on Jesus did was to lead Him into the desert to be tempted by Satan. This does not mean that the Spirit and the devil were in cahoots to get Jesus to do evil; for the word tempt can also mean to test or prove. God by His Spirit was directing Jesus to face profound spiritual testing. In this, Jesus repeated in a personal way the kind of testing Israel faced as God's "son" during the 40 years in the wilderness (see Deut. 6—8). That national "son" failed the tests repeatedly but Jesus here triumphed in His.

The fast on which Jesus embarked for 40 days and 40 nights was probably not absolute. He probably allowed Himself drink, but no solid food. That would leave Him weak, even emaciated, but still alive and alert.

The manner in which the devil approached Him is not clear. The trip to a very high mountain (Matt. 4:8) was certainly visionary, since no mountain can provide a natural vantage point for seeing all of the world's kingdoms. Whatever form Satan took, his attack was personal and subtle, and focused on three areas.

First, the devil picked up on the testimony the Father had just given to Jesus (3:17) and said, in effect, that if Jesus was truly the Father's Son, He should display His power by turning the stones into bread in order to satisfy His own hunger. After all, what father would begrudge his own son food, especially if it was within the son's power to gain it? Why should God the Father object to that?

Jesus' response, quoting Deuteronomy 8:3, showed that Satan was really trying to incite Jesus to move away from a notion of sonship that involved strict conformity to God's every word (see Matt. 4:4). Obedience to God's every word was to Jesus more necessary than sustaining food.

But there is more. We must conclude that if Jesus had used the powers rightly His, He would have been *disobeying* the Father's commands to Him about His mission. If He had acted powerfully on His own behalf, He would have overturned the self-abasement that was an essential part of His mission; He would not have learned obedience through suffering (see Heb. 3:5,6; 5:7,8).

The temptation was similar to the one that would be hurled at Him by the crowds in Matthew 27:40: "Come down from the cross, if you are the Son of God!" How easy for Him to do so— but then the very purpose of His coming would have been destroyed.

The *second* temptation finds the devil quoting and misapplying Scripture. The Old Testament promises that God will protect those who trust Him (Ps. 91:11,12). So if Jesus was the Son of God, the devil argued, He should test this supported intimacy with His Father against God's pledge to protect His own.

Jesus did not wish to enter into disputes over His Father's love for Him or God's willingness and ability to protect Him. Rather, He recognized that behind Satan's challenge was an invitation to approach God with a kind of emotional blackmail, a twisted spiritual bribery. Scripture flatly forbids the believer such conduct (see Deut. 6:16, which Jesus quotes). God's watch-care over His people does not give them the right to treat God with cheap presumption. Their attitude must be trust and obedience (see Deut. 6:17).

The *third* temptation was an invitation to achieve kingly power in a shortcut, by worshiping God's archenemy. According to Satan, Jesus could gain full authority over the world by sidestepping the cross and taking up idolatry. But Jesus recognized that this was the most appalling sin. Neither Israel the national "son," nor Jesus Himself, nor anyone else, may deviate from undivided allegiance to God without stooping to the blackest paganism, for it is written, "Worship the Lord your God, and serve Him only" (Matt. 4:10, quoting Deut. 6:13).

And so this period of acute temptation passed, but it was not the only time when Jesus would confront and expose Satan's wiles. (See Matt. 16:21-23 and compare to Luke 4:13.)

Jesus' Expanding Ministry

Like Mark and Luke, Matthew made no mention that Jesus' ministry in Judea overlapped that of the Baptist (see also John 2:13—3:21). But unless we suppose that John the Baptist was arrested and imprisoned immediately after baptizing Jesus, Matthew 4:12 implies some sort of delay; for there we are told that Jesus withdrew to Galilee only after the arrest of the one who had baptized Him.

That is where Matthew picked up the story. One of the reasons for Matthew's silence about the earlier period is that he wanted to move immediately to another prophecy about Messiah's ministry, a prophecy touching the Gentiles. Quoted from Isaiah 9:1-2, the prophecy in Matthew 4:15,16 focuses on Galilee, a region known for its relatively high concentration of Gentiles. Even there, the prophet tells us, the light had dawned. It was there, in the ancient tribal territories of Zebulun and Naphtali, that Jesus preached, settling in the Galilean town of Capernaum, bringing to fulfillment the ancient text.

Formally, the message Jesus preached—summarized in the

line, "Repent, for the kingdom of heaven is near" (Matt. 4:17)—
is identical with the summary of John the Baptist's preaching
(3:2). Nevertheless, there is a subtle difference between these
two summaries, imposed on them by their respective contexts.

This difference is made possible by the ambiguity of the verb
used in the phrase "for the kingdom of heaven *is near.*" This
could mean either that the kingdom was impending and would
soon be there, even though it had not yet arrived *or* that the
kingdom was already close, nearer than anyone had thought.
When John the Baptist preached this message, he did so *as the
forerunner who was preparing the way for someone else.* So "is
near" in that context took on the flavor of the *first* meaning. But
when Jesus preached the same message, He was set in the role
not of a forerunner, but of the one whose ministry was *already*
shedding light on the Gentiles. So, in reference to Jesus, "is
near" takes on some of the flavor of the *second* meaning.

This is entirely in accord with a major theme in Matthew.
Although a majority of the passages in Matthew that say something about the kingdom are referring to the final kingdom at the
end of the age, a significant number of them insist that the kingdom came at the time of Jesus' ministry. For instance, in Matthew 12:28 Jesus insists that if He could drive out demons by the
Spirit of God, then the kingdom of God *had come* upon the people. This careful tension between a kingdom that is *not yet* here
and a kingdom that is *already* here—even though it is the *same*
kingdom that is being discussed—is what makes many Christians talk about a *future* kingdom and an *inaugurated* kingdom.

This theme has many parallels. For instance, the New Testament tells us that true Christians *already have* eternal life (as in
John 5:24) but it also tells us that we *will inherit* eternal life at
the end of the age (as in Matt. 25:46). We have *already* been justified by God's grace but our final transformation to become a
just people has not yet occurred. In one sense we have already
passed from death to life but we wait for Jesus' return before we
receive our resurrection bodies and perfect freedom from every
trace of death. In exactly the same way, the preaching of Jesus
demanding repentance on the grounds that the kingdom was
near announced something *present* about the kingdom, precisely

because His preaching was set in the context of Messianic *fulfill-ment.*

Our final glimpses of Jesus in this chapter are two. First, we find Him gathering an inner ring of disciples (4:18-22) whom He promised to train as evangelists (fishers of men). This step may have been facilitated by earlier dealings with these men (compare to John 1:35-42) but in any case it proves Jesus envisaged a long haul that would require workers, not an immediate, cataclysmic finish.

Second, in the last vignette we see just how busy an itinerant preacher, teacher, and healer Jesus was. The first-century historian Josephus tells us there were more than two hundred cities and villages in Galilee, each with more than 15,000 people. Even if Josephus was high in his estimates, a preacher who stopped at two communities a day would require more than three months to visit them all—with no days off for Sabbath! The sheer emotional drain must have been fantastic as Jesus' fame multiplied. Week after week He taught in their synagogues, preached "the good news of the kingdom" (what it was about and that it was near), healed many people, and exorcised many demons in powerful displays of the dawning kingdom's transforming power.

Questions for Further Study

1. If the good news of Jesus' first advent and ministry served as the grounds for repentance, in what ways should the good news of Jesus' future return serve as the grounds for our repentance today?

2. What modern temptations do we face that parallel the three Jesus confronted in Matthew 4:1-11?

3. What areas of our lives are we most likely to exclude from the all-embracing sweep of repentance? What would John the Baptist say to such shallow repentance?

4. List all the verses in the first four chapters of Matthew in

which some hope is held out for Gentiles.

5. List all the quotations from the Old Testament referred to so far. Keep a running list.

6. How does Matthew 4:18-22 bear on us today? Compare those verses to Matthew 28:18-20.

Some subjects seem to attract a lot of discussion. Pretty soon so much has been written on the subject that others begin writing just to describe what has been written.

That's the way it is with the Sermon on the Mount. Thousands and thousands of books and essays have devoted themselves to these three chapters of Matthew's Gospel. The output is so great that several long books have been written to survey this vast literature and explain the various "camps" or "schools" that approach the Sermon in distinctive ways.

So one short chapter in a very small book can do no more than to sketch in with broad strokes the author's understanding of the Sermon on the Mount. But the wealth of material in these chapters of Matthew is so rich that Christians really hungry to know more about the Bible and about what God thinks could do a lot worse than to pause here and memorize Matthew 5—7, and then move on to longer expositions and commentaries in order to get to know this Sermon well. Hiding this part of God's Word in our hearts is guaranteed to transform our thinking and living.

In one sense, of course, these chapters do not provide a full record of a sermon. They take about ten minutes to read; and it is unlikely that Jesus withdrew to the hills, attracted a crowd, and then spoke for only ten minutes! Some of His excursions turned into three-day conferences (see Matt. 15:32). These three chapters are condensed reports of long teaching sessions and are therefore necessarily selective and topical.

It appears that Jesus originally intended to teach this material only *to His disciples*, not to the crowds. He observed the crowds (4:23-25; 5:1) and withdrew from them to the hills, where His disciples congregated around him. Nevertheless, we must notice two details if this picture is not to distort our understanding of the Sermon on the Mount.

First, the term disciples does not mean, at this early stage of Jesus' public ministry, only the Twelve, who are not introduced until chapter 10. Nor does it mean Christians in the full, post-Pentecost sense. None of those who early placed their faith in Jesus really understood that He, the Messiah, would have to suffer and die as a sacrifice for sin. Yet there were many who followed Him, sought to follow His teachings, and regarded themselves as His disciples—just as those who followed John the Baptist saw themselves as the Baptist's disciples (see 11:2). This more committed group Jesus intended to teach and train.

But *second,* so great was His rising popularity that by the end of this conference there were great crowds who were listening in (see 7:28,29)—just as later on it was extraordinarily difficult for Him to escape their attention (see 14:13,14).

The reason these two points are important to a fair understanding of the Sermon on the Mount is this: these chapters include not only material suitable for those who really are Jesus' disciples ("You are the salt of the earth," 5:13; see also 5:14; 7:7-11) but also warnings aimed at those who think they are true disciples but aren't (see 7:21-23).

Some passages provide challenge (6:24,33) and even invitation (7:13,14). Those who were His disciples needed to press on with their discipleship, deepen their understanding and commitment, and enter into a relationship of obedience and transformed living (6:19-34; 7:15-23) that would not only mark them out as distinct from the surrounding culture but would also continue after Jesus Messiah had died and risen again.

And, those who were not yet disciples in any sense, but who had rushed into the hills like gate-crashers and joined the "teach-in," stood in no less need of such fundamental challenge. Thus the Sermon on the Mount, for all that it is a block of teaching, is not reserved, formal, or merely didactic. It is also a call to repentance, obedience, and faith.

The Norms and Witness of the Kingdom

Diligent readers often cherish writers and speakers who can capture a complex position in a single, polished gem of a statement. Such aphorisms (as they are called) are especially telling when they first become public.

Unfortunately, once an aphorism has been widely disseminated, it is in danger of being domesticated—a trained poodle that is dragged out when the circumstances require it. For many Christians, that is what has become of the Beatitudes (literally, the blessings, a name derived from the first word of each verse). We are so familiar with them that the words can glide piously off our tongues without disturbing us. Yet each of these beatitudes is a *revolutionary* aphorism and together they can, when properly understood, utterly overthrow secularism and radically transform insipid Christianity.

The first (5:3) insists that the really "blessed" people—those who have God's approval—are those who are "poor in spirit." Those who are so approved by God that they inherit His kingdom are not the spiritual elite, the morally influential, the prayerful mystics—but the spiritually destitute. The ones who enjoy the kingdom are not these who can display the greatest spiritual growth or credentials, but those who file for spiritual bankruptcy. The kingdom is not for the person who makes a profession of faith as if such a step is doing God a favor, but for the person who constantly recognizes the impoverished state of his or her life, and approaches God on no other ground than that of need.

The last beatitude in the series (5:10) is no less startling. The kingdom of heaven is promised, as a function of God's blessing or approval, not to the successful witness, the towering pillar of rectitude, the globe-trotting Christian leader—but to "those who are persecuted because of righteousness . . . . " This person's conduct is so righteous the world cannot stand it.

The picture is not of a holier-than-thou goody-goody, but of a believer stamped with *integrity*—integrity in commerce, speech, personal transactions, filing income tax forms, providing value for money, relationships with the opposite sex, integrity everywhere and at all times. The world usually prefers a veneer of integrity or integrity in select areas. When it meets the real thing, it reacts with revulsion.

In one sense this has always been so. Even in the Old Testament, God addressed the righteous people of Isaiah's day in these terms: "Hear me, you who know what is right, you people who have my law in your hearts: Do not fear the reproach of men or be terrified by their insults" (Isaiah 51:7).

Indeed, this beatitude is so important that it is expanded in the next two verses (Matt. 5:11,12—with a change from third person to second—you—to make the challenge more direct). Now it becomes clear that the persecution of 5:10 would include insults and slander.

But although it has always been true that genuinely righteous people do not win popularity contests, there is an extra sting in this case. In verse 10, Jesus said that the reason for the persecution is "because of righteousness." Now He further explained that persecution would come "because of me" (5:11). In other words, the righteousness that is in view is that which arises out of a person's discipleship to Jesus.

There is a further and rather startling implication: disciples of Jesus who are persecuted align themselves with the prophets of old who were persecuted (5:12). As the prophets lived in allegiance to God and paid a social price, we must live in allegiance to Jesus and pay a social price. But that means we are parallel to the prophets, and Jesus is parallel to God. It seems that the more we meditate on this beatitude, the more it becomes not only a challenge but a veiled messianic claim.

Yet challenge it is—fully in line with other New Testament passages that warn the follower of Jesus to expect opposition and that almost make it a badge of genuine faith and discipleship (see Luke 6:26; John 15:18—6:4; Acts 14:22; 2 Tim. 3:12; 1 Pet. 4:13,14). Easy believism may be comfortable with the world and pop philosophy such as the "power of positive thinking" phrased in evangelical cliches may win worldly acclaim, but Jesus' true disciples will win some flak. On the other hand, they and they alone will discover that "theirs is the kingdom of heaven" (Matt. 5:10).

This blessing is the same as that promised in the *first* beatitude (5:3). All the rest are different (5:4-9). Beginning and ending a section of writing with the same theme and even the same words is a stylistic device that the literary critics call an inclusion, a kind of literary envelope. In this instance it means that all the norms set forth in the Beatitudes have to do with inheriting the kingdom of heaven. They are, if you like, the norms of the kingdom.

It is not possible to go through them in detail in this short chapter but perhaps we may savor one verse. Verse 6 promises God's blessing on those "who hunger and thirst for righteousness." Hunger and thirst represent the deepest desires (see also Ps. 42:2). Certainly the deepest famine is hunger for the Word of God (see Amos 8:11-14). Jesus' disciples passionately desire righteousness not only that they may wholly do God's will from the heart but more, that they may see righteousness everywhere. (In Matthew, the word *righteousness* never takes on the meaning *imputed righteousness* as it often does in Paul's writings.) All unrighteousness and injustice grieves them and makes them homesick for the new heaven and the new earth, the home of righteousness (see 2 Pet. 3:13). God's blessing on them is to fill them with righteousness in measure now, without limit one day.

Clearly, the values set forth in the Beatitudes are fundamentally different from those of the central areas of modern life, education, technological development, or military might. The astonishing thing is that many people, because they are vaguely familiar with them, actually think they are more or less living them. Cheap familiarity has robbed these aphorisms of their force. But renewed reflection on them not only highlights their transcendent moral stature, but forces us to examine ourselves (see 2 Cor. 13:5) to discover if we ourselves are heirs of the kingdom.

Certainly those who live by such norms cannot do so in secret. Theirs is not a religion of private experience only, but also of *public* integrity, meekness, righteousness, purity, and mercy. That is why the next verses immediately move on to consider the witness of the kingdom (Matt. 5:12-16).

The theme of witnessing is laid out in two metaphors. The first pictures Jesus' followers as *salt* (5:13-16). In the ancient near East, though salt was used for many things, it was primarily used as a preservative. In the days before refrigerators, salting down meat was the best way to preserve it. Much of this salt came from salt marshes and the like and, therefore, had many impurities. If such salt were leached a little, the percentage of impurities could become so high that the salt would have no effectiveness. So also are Jesus' followers to retard decay in a world that drifts constantly toward corruption. But if they are leached, removing what is distinctive about them, they are useless. They certainly do not staunch the world's evil if they lose their distinctive obedience, allegiance, and power. In fact, in time they are simply trampled underfoot.

Or to put it another way (5:15,16), just as a city on a hill, lighted at night by a thousand shimmering olive oil lamps, cannot be hidden, so a true disciple of Jesus cannot be hidden. Such people will stand out. And in any case, just as it is ridiculous to light a lamp and then hide it under a measuring bowl, so it is unthinkable to hide the Christian's light. The very *purpose* of the lamp is to shed light in a dark place; and the very *purpose* of Jesus' followers is to shed the light of Jesus, of biblical revelation, of moral integrity, of the gospel of the kingdom, in a very dark world.

Jesus' Relation to the Old Testament

The main body of the Sermon on the Mount runs from Matthew 5:17 to 7:12; and again, we find an inclusion, a literary envelope, in that the beginning and ending verses mention the law and the prophets. This suggests that Jesus, in the body of the Sermon on the Mount, was explaining the relationship between His teaching and the Old Testament Scriptures—which were sometimes called "the law and the prophets," sometimes simply "the law" (as in 5:18), and sometimes "the law, the prophets and the psalms" (see Luke 24:44).

The exact nature of the relationship that Jesus spelled out turns in large part on the interpretation of Matthew 5:17-20. In particular, the relationship focuses on the force of the word fulfill. Some have noted that 5:17 sets the verbs abolish and fulfill against each other—Jesus has not come to *abolish* the law but to *fulfill* it—and conclude that to fulfill in this context must mean to keep, preserve, even intensify.

The problem with such an interpretation is that Matthew elsewhere seems to say that certain parts of the Old Testament law were *not* applicable any longer *as law*; and certainly other New Testament writers make this clear in various ways (see Heb. 8:13; 9:6-10). Few Christians, for instance, follow the Old Testament food laws anymore (see Matt. 15:1-20) and none of us offers sacrifices at a temple in Jerusalem. So in *some* sense, Old Testament laws *have* been abolished. Others have argued that in Matthew 5:17 Jesus must therefore have been referring only to *moral* law. But this view is contradicted by 5:18 which, far from restricting the law to its moral component, insists that what is being discussed includes *all* of it, right down to the tiniest letter and the crossing if a *t*. This not only reflects Jesus' immensely high valuation of the truthfulness of the Old Testament but, more important, it rules out any restriction of subject matter to just one part of the law.

The best approach is to appreciate that Matthew used the word fulfill exactly as he had already used it (see chapter 1 of this book). The word does not here mean to keep, preserve, or intensify but to *fulfill* as an event *fulfills* prediction and prophecy. We have already learned that some prophecies are not simple predictions but may include events and people that serve as "types" of what is coming in the future.

In short, Jesus was saying that the purpose of His coming, ministry, and message was not *to abolish* the Scriptures already given (what we today call the Old Testament), but *to serve as that to which those Scriptures point*. Jesus assumed that those

Scriptures were broadly prophetic, both law and prophets. As He said elsewhere the law and the prophets *prophesied* until the time of John the Baptist (11:13). Jesus refused to see the Scriptures already given as the conveyor of a perpetually definitive *revelation of law as such,* but primarily as a prophetic revelation.

The continuing authority of those Scriptures, therefore, rests primarily in that to which they point, in the authority of the person and ministry they have prophesied. *Everything* those Scriptures have prophesied will be accomplished; nothing will fall to the ground, thwarted and frustrated, till the end of time, "till heaven and earth disappear" until one-by-one each detail that has been prophesied takes place, "until everything is accomplished" (5:18).

It is *in that sense* that even the least of the Old Testament commandments must still be practiced and not broken (5:19). The disciples of Jesus practice all the commandments when—in the new situation prophesied of old and now brought about by the person, ministry, death, and resurrection of Jesus—they adhere to and practice all that this new revelation demands, precisely because it *fulfills* the older revelation. It is that to which the older revelation pointed.

The way this works out for at least some parts of the law is evident from the rest of the chapter (5:21-48). These verses are often summed up as the six antitheses, because Jesus began each of the six separate sections with some variation of "You have heard that it was said . . . but I say" (5:21, 27,31,33,38,43).

Part of what the people had heard was the Scripture—what we call the Old Testament—but part of what they had heard, though they thought it had scriptural authority, was misinformed interpretation. For example, they rightly heard that Scripture taught, "Love your neighbor" (5:43; see also Lev. 19:18). But some authorities reasoned, "It says *neighbor* so that means we do not need to love an enemy. Indeed, there is implicit sanction to hate an enemy." So what some people had heard, therefore, was "Love your neighbor and hate your enemy" (Matt. 5:43).

Jesus would have nothing to do with such casuistry. He insisted, "Love your enemies and pray for those who persecute you, that you may be sons of your Father in heaven. He causes his sun to rise on the evil and the good, and sends rain on the righteous and the unrighteous" (5:44,45). "To return evil for good is devilish; to return good for good is human; to return good for evil is divine."[1] Any old pagan can love friends and greet brothers; but the followers of Jesus must transcend such standards. After all, as Broadus puts it, "In loving his friends a man may in a certain sense be loving only himself—a kind of expanded selfishness."[2]

Yet in light of Matthew 5:17-20 and the theme of how Jesus *fulfills* the Scriptures, we must not think that the antithesis in 5:43-48 was simply offering Jesus' private interpretation of the Old Testament, and no more. Rather, He was saying that His own teaching was the true direction in which the Scriptures point.

Perhaps this is even clearer in His antithesis on oaths (5:33-37). In this case, Jesus *formally* abrogated something the Old Testament commends and regulates. The problem rested in the perverse interpretations that permitted evasive oaths that didn't have to be kept—like the child who swears, "Cross my heart and hope to die!" but believes it doesn't count because she has her fingers crossed behind her back! Her oath is just a clever excuse to lie convincingly. A later passage in Matthew provides some fine examples of evasive oaths (23:16-22). But the real direction in which the Old Testament laws on oaths point is toward perfect truth-telling. That means, Jesus authoritatively insisted that if it was necessary to abolish the regulations on oaths, and even oaths themselves, for the sake of truth He was happy to do so.

A central problem in wrestling with the ethics of Jesus is our dismal rush to ask questions of the form, "What does this mean we can get away with?" But however the details of these antitheses are interpreted, surely it is clear that their *thrust* condemns such a question as perverse. We often want to know who our neighbor is, not because we clamor to please God but because we want to circumscribe our responsibility and minimize our guilt and failure. We may struggle with a text that tells us to gouge out our right eye (5:29) not so much because we are all wooden literalists as because the image so strongly insists we deal radically with lust.

But these verses will not let us escape so lightly. At their heart is a fiery demand for a purity, a holiness, a righteousness that outstrips all pretense and condemns cheap casuistry. That is why the section ends with the shattering demand, "Be perfect, therefore, as your heavenly Father is perfect" (5:48). The true direction in which the law and prophets pointed, and the ethical heart of the kingdom the Lord Jesus preached and introduced, is the moral perfection of God Himself.

What this Means—and Doesn't Mean

An astonishing proof of human perversity is to be found in our remarkable ability to transform high moral tone into legalistic self-righteousness and moral smugness. When I was at university twenty years ago, Christians were sometimes exhorted to carry their Bibles with them. It was such a small measure of witness and, besides, if campus Communists were proud to be carrying some of the writings of Marx under their arms, why shouldn't Christians be delighted to carry the Bible? True enough. But it was not long before a few Christians turned carrying a Bible into a test for spiritual zeal. It almost seemed as if they thought spiritual fervor was directly proportionate to the size of the Bible displayed.

There are many such examples. In the Korean church there is a long and healthy tradition of spiritual retreats. Christian leaders take time off to go to a secluded place to fast and pray. But some wise Koreans have recently voiced concern over the ostentation with which some leaders carry out this regular pilgrimage. In other circles, justifiable interest in Christian dress and deportment can easily degenerate into detailed rules that are accorded the authority of Scripture itself.

Jesus was never naive in His preaching and teaching. Accordingly, when He made the astonishing demands of Matthew 5:43-48, He knew they could easily be prostituted into cheap rules that would miss a large part of what He was demanding. Therefore He proceeded in the next verses to warn against the kind of religion that confuses ostentation with devotion, that is less in love with godliness and holiness than with a *reputation* for godliness and holiness.

In Matthew 6:1-18, Jesus focused on three dominant practices in Jewish piety of the first century: giving to the needy (vv. 2-4), praying (vv. 5-15), and fasting (vv. 16-18). In each case, the heart of the warning was that acts of piety must *never* be done out of a desire to win the praise of others (see also John 5:44; 12:43). Those who stoop to such motives may indeed win human applause; but that is all they get—"they have received their reward in full" (Matt. 6:2,5,16). Their acts of piety have no significance at all so far as God is concerned.

The proper way to avoid such traps is to practice a great deal of piety *in private*. People should not learn about our acts of kindness and our generous gifts—especially not from us! And we may be quite sure our piety does not amount to much if our public praying is the bulk of our total prayer life, rather than a tiny part of the overflow of our secret praying. Fasting likewise becomes worthless once it has become public and regulated.

It is important to recognize that Jesus did not rule out giving, praying, and fasting. Quite the contrary. He seemed rather to expect such things in His followers. But He wanted such steps to be taken as gifts freely offered up, in secret, to the heavenly Father. This would guarantee that our discipleship to Jesus Christ is neither legalism nor ostentation, but the honest adoration, worship, and obedience of a life given over to the Lord Jesus and to His heavenly Father.

In the second of three examples, dealing with prayer, Jesus provided a model of the right kind of prayer (vv. 9-13). The first three petitions focus on God's name, God's kingdom, and God's will; the last three focus on our physical needs, our sins (often seen as debts), and our temptations.

This is not the only model prayer in Scripture (see, for instance, 1 Kings 8:23-53; Eph. 3:14-21) but it is the model prayer the Lord Himself left for us, and who better knew how to pray?

Jesus' warnings against babbling on like pagans (Matt. 6:7,8) must be balanced by what He said elsewhere about persevering prayer (see Luke 18:1-8). The former warning is directed against those who think they are heard for their much speaking and the latter against those whose spiritual fervor is so low they show little passion to know God. The simplicity and profundity of this model prayer deserve prolonged meditation and thoughtful emulation.

These negative lessons about ostentation can be put more positively into succinct principles. The *first* is this: Get your affections on eternal things, not the material world (Matt. 6:19-24). Some people say there is a danger that Christians will become so heavenly-minded they'll be no earthly good. The Bible's perspective is far different. It argues that those who are truly most heavenly-minded will be good for both heaven and earth. Those with their values in heaven will *care* about integrity, humility, proper relationships, motive, and love *on earth*. Those who do not have such values will gradually be corrupted by power or money, or will set their hopes on transient goods that can only disappoint those who idolize them.

The *second* principle is this: Practice trust in the sovereign goodness of God, and do not worry even about necessities, since He pledged to care for His own (Matt. 6:25-34; Rom. 8:28). One responsibility is to seek His kingdom and righteousness, confident that He will supply the necessities (Matt. 6:33).

There are two other dangers that confront those who pursue righteousness. The first is a judgmental attitude (7:1-5) and the second, ironically, is a refusal to use any judgment at all (7:6). The first sin occurs in disciples who are not only legalistic but somewhat proud of the progress they have made. They are eager to set everybody else straight, and become blind to their own considerable failures. The other sin occurs in those who so much take to heart the commands to love people that they forget what else Jesus said about human beings—our wickedness, deception, malice, cruelty. As a result, they become undiscerning goody-goodies who not only lack sense but ultimately get trampled in the mud.

Far better is it to recognize our need for constant help in all these areas, and go humbly to our heavenly Father and *ask*, *seek*, and *knock* (7:7-12). Good Father that He is, God is always ready to give genuinely good gifts to those who ask Him. So frequently we lack His marvelous supply simply because we either fail to ask, or ask with corrupt motives (see James 4:2,3).

And meanwhile, if we need a rule of thumb to understand just how the Old Testament—the law and the prophets—should work out in our lives, Jesus provided us with the golden rule: "In everything, do to others what you would have them do to you, for this sums up the Law and the Prophets" (Matt. 7:12).

Other teachers have sometimes taught a *negative* form of the golden rule: "Do *not* do to others what you would *not* want them to do to you." But Jesus will not let us get off so easily. The goats in Matthew 25:31-46 could squeak through under the negative rule, but not under the positive. Jesus went after sins of omission as well as sins of commission. However, Jesus was not offering a maxim like "Honesty pays"—as if He was telling us to act in a kind way so that others will be kind to us in turn. Nor is it dreamy wishfulness, like much radical humanism. Far from it. We are to obey this rule *because* such conduct sums up the Scriptures already given.

The Alternatives

The Sermon on the Mount ends with four warnings, each of which offers a pair of contrasts and the need to choose: two ways (7:13,14), two trees (7:15-20), two claims (7:21-23), and two builders (7:24-27). Few passages stress the centrality of obedience more powerfully than these verses. The so-called follower of Jesus who never enters the narrow way, who brings forth bad fruit, who says, "Lord, Lord" to Jesus but never practices the will of the Father—in short, who builds his or her life on no firm foundation—will one day be dismissed forever from Christ's presence as an "evildoer" (7:23). No one can leave behind a study of the Sermon on the Mount without facing these alternatives and recognizing that one's eternal destiny hangs on them.

The Sermon on the Mount must not simply be studied, but practiced and incorporated into the believer's life. Failure to make progress in this regard calls into doubt the validity of the individual's claims to be following Jesus at all. Conversely, the person who experiences the power of God's reign in his or her life, and as a result finds that obedience to Jesus and delight in God's will are the most cherished things in all the world, not only produces good fruit now (7:16-18) and cheerfully walks the narrow way (7:13,14), but on the day when all people everywhere face the storm of God's wrath, delights in the security of a firm foundation (7:24-27).

Notes
1. Alfred Plummer, *An Exegetical Commentary on the Gospel According to St. Matthew* (London: Robert Scott, 1915).
2. John Broadus, *Commentary on the Gospel of Matthew* (Valley Forge: American Baptist Publication Society, 1886).

Questions for Further Study

1. How can the "norms of the kingdom" (5:3-12) be nurtured and fostered in our daily lives?

2. In what ways should we be as salt and light in the specific contexts in which we live?

3. Does Matthew 5:33-37 mean Christians should not take oaths in court? Justify your answer.

4. Does Matthew 5:38-47 mean Christians should not serve in police or military forces? Justify your answer.

5. What tendencies toward religious hypocrisy, parallel to those in Matthew 6:1-18, abound in our circles? How can we best overcome them?

6. Why do many Christians contravene Matthew 6:25-34 and worry and fret constantly? What responses does the Sermon on the Mount give to such fretting?

7. In practical terms, what do the concluding alternatives (Matt. 7:13-27) mean we should do? What concrete changes in our lives are demanded?

Miracles and Mission 4

In many modern biographies, the writer proceeds chronologically through the subject's life. But that is not the only way of writing a biography. In Antonia Fraser's magnificent biography of *Cromwell: Our Chief of Men,* the author follows a chronological pattern until Cromwell becomes Lord Protector; and then she switches to a topical treatment of Cromwell's rule.

The four Gospel writers followed a roughly chronological pattern in their treatment of Jesus, at least as far as certain major events in His life were concerned. His baptism at the hands of John the Baptist preceded His public ministry; His preaching, miracles, and claims provoked rising opposition; His life was climaxed by His death and resurrection. Yet by comparing the four Gospels, it becomes immediately clear that the accounts are very often topical in their arrangement.

That means that if we pay close attention to how various stories about Jesus are linked in one Gospel, even when the same stories are told in a different sequence in another Gospel, we can sometimes gain valuable insights into the particular themes and topics being emphasized. None of the Gospels, and certainly not Matthew's, is a result of a random or haphazard throwing together of stories that don't cohere. There is always a pattern, topical or chronological—and often several skillfully interwoven patterns can be detected at the same time.

So it is here. The Sermon on the Mount ended with the crowds amazed at Jesus' authority (Matt 7:28,29). Now Matthew provided a number of accounts in which various facets of Jesus' authority were demonstrated (chapters 8-9), and these are climaxed by Jesus conferring some of His authority (10:1) on the twelve, who were then sent out in a trainee mission (10:5-42).

Jesus' Authority in His Miracles

Much of the demonstration of Jesus' authority comes in the form of accounts of His miracles. But these are not piled one on top of another to make the one point and nothing more. Rather, each account, while stressing Jesus' authority, provides important insight into the nature of Jesus' person, demands, and ministry.

In the first, Jesus healed a man with a skin disease (what the Bible calls leprosy)—a disease that not only made a person an outcast but which often served as a symbol for sin's intractable power. The law of Moses forbade anyone from touching a leper; but when Jesus formally broke this law (8:3), far from becoming unclean Himself, He made the unclean clean. In some sense, therefore, Jesus demonstrated His power over law.

The silence Jesus then enjoined here and elsewhere in Matthew (8:4; 9:30; 12:16; 17:9) was probably motivated by Jesus' constant desire not to present Himself as a mere wonder-worker. Wonder-workers draw crowds—but not always repentance and faith. But the most telling stroke in the account is Jesus' insistence that the healed man should follow the law's prescriptions for lepers who claimed to be cured by going to Jerusalem and showing himself to a priest (8:4; see also Lev. 14), and offering the stipulated sacrifice. All this, Jesus said, was "as a testimony to them."

This is profoundly insightful. On the one hand, Jesus transcended the law's prohibition against touching lepers, but could not be charged because His touch destroyed the evidence; and on the other hand, He minutely followed the law of Moses in its statutes on cured lepers, knowing that the priest would have to declare the former leper healed—and this judgment would reflect on Jesus' power and authority.

In both cases, the law pointed to Jesus and the gospel. In the former, its distinctions between clean and unclean made it clear how important "cleanness" is to God and anticipated God's decisive initiative in making the unclean clean. In the latter, obedience to the law of Moses became the occasion for the law to confirm the authority of Jesus, who needed only to will the deed for it to be done.

The next miracle to be recounted, the healing of the centurion's servant (8:5-13), again stressed Jesus' authority—and this time, He healed at a distance, by word only, without touch. But in addition there are two other themes that emerge rather strongly from these verses, themes Matthew made as central to his Gospel.

The *first* theme is faith. Jesus was frankly astonished at the centurion's faith. That faith presented itself most strongly in the reason the soldier advanced for Jesus not to bother coming but just to say a healing word. The soldier made his reason clear by an analogy. Because of the hierarchical nature of the Roman military, when a centurion barked an order it was not merely the will of one man being imposed on another. Far from it. Precisely because the centurion was part of a large authority structure, when the centurion spoke Rome spoke. If a foot soldier disobeyed, he would face the judgment not only of an individual centurion but of the Roman government with all its might. And that was why a centurion need only say, "Do this"—and it was done.

Applying this analogy to Jesus, the centurion was saying in effect that he perceived Jesus to stand in a similar authority relationship—but with God, not Rome. When Jesus spoke, therefore, God spoke. And because this was so, Jesus needed only to say the word for the healing to be effected. Such farsighted and understanding faith is rare in the Gospels; but the importance of faith is stressed by Matthew, and reappears a little later in another Gentile (15:21-28).

And that brings us to the *second* theme: Gentiles are here welcomed into the messianic community. One day they will sit down at the final messianic banquet, along with the great Jewish fathers—Abraham, Isaac, and Jacob (8:11). Sadly, some who by race might have expected an inside track will find themselves excluded. Matthew has already stressed the Gentile theme (see chapters 1 and 2 of this book) and now once more he reported how the ground was prepared for the Great Commission. After Pentecost, another centurion would come to faith, and his conversion would force the church to recognize this truth: "So then, God has even granted the Gentiles repentance unto life" (Acts 11:18).

Other miracles in these chapters convey more than mere miracle as well. In the calming of the storm (8:23-27), Jesus demonstrated not only His power over nature, but returned again to the theme of *faith* (8:25,26). His rebuke did not reflect spiritual naiveté—as if no followers of Jesus could ever drown in a storm. It was the manifestation of their unbelief in their *fear* that won them the sharp criticism. At very least the disciples should have committed themselves to the heavenly Father in loving trust—especially after hearing the Sermon on the Mount (especially 6:25-34)! But a faith that was *really* perceptive should also have recognized, as a hymn-writer put it:

No water can swallow the ship where lies
The Master of ocean, and earth, and skies . . . ![1]

That is why the section ends as it does—with a wondering focus on the "kind of man" this Jesus is (8:27). Moreover, to the reader who thinks hard about the juxtaposition of human frailties and divine authority in the one person Jesus the account is profound: "As Jesus is tempted but rebukes Satan (4:1-11), as he is called the devil but casts out demons (12:22-32), so he sleeps from weariness but muzzles nature."[2]

In the healing of the two demon-possessed men (8:28-34), we perceive Jesus' authority over evil spirits. Recognized by the spirit world (8:29), Jesus was addressed in such a way that we are again reminded He is the final judge. The words "Have you come here to torture us before the appointed time?" (8:29) recall 7:21-23.

Meanwhile the account also shows that the people in the area preferred pigs above seeing these men released, swine above the Saviour. These people were Gentiles, judging by the region and the presence of pigs—no Jew would have kept them! Just as being a Jew does not guarantee a place in the messianic kingdom (3:9; 8:11,12), so being a Gentile is no guarantee either. What counts is a response of obedient faith to Jesus the Messiah.

The account of the healing of the paralytic (9:1-8) makes the theme of Jesus' authority explicit. The crowds praised God who gave such *authority* to men (9:8). But again a new wealth of meaning is introduced; for Jesus insisted that He has authority not only to heal but to forgive sins—a prerogative of God alone (9:2,5,6).

This same emphasis is related to 8:14-17 where, after healing Peter's mother-in-law, Jesus healed and exorcised many afflicted people. Matthew concluded that this was done to fulfill the prophecy of Isaiah 53:4. The suffering servant, Isaiah said, "took up our infirmities and carried our diseases" (8:17). Other parts of the New Testament make it clear that the *way* Jesus as the suffering servant bore our infirmities and diseases was through His death on the cross (see Acts 8:32,33; 1 Peter 2:24). So why should Matthew say that Jesus' healing miracles, not His death, fulfilled this prophecy from Isaiah?

The question can be answered if we remember three things. *First,* the Scriptures everywhere presuppose a tight connection between sin and sickness. This does not mean that every sickness is the direct result of a particular sin (see John 9:2,3) though some sickness may be (see John 5:14). But it does mean that all sickness derives from our fallenness. If we had never rebelled against God, there would never have been any sickness or death. That is why, in the new heaven and new earth, where there is no more sin, sickness and death are also abolished (see Rev. 21:4,27; 22:3).

Second, the fundamental means God has graciously provided for removing our *sin* is the sacrificial death and triumphant resurrection of Jesus; and therefore the fundamental means God has provided for removing our *sickness* is the sacrificial death and triumphant resurrection of Jesus. Indeed, every blessing that comes our way is in some sense related to the cross-work of Jesus Christ; for without this sacrifice God provided on our behalf, God's justice would have demanded that our rebellious race be wiped out.

It is therefore quite correct to say, for instance, that there is healing in the atonement—a slogan in many Christian circles. But in the same sense, there is also a resurrection body and a new heaven and a new earth in the atonement. All these benefits have been secured for believers by the atonement. That does not mean I can expect to claim my resurrection body *now*, simply because it has been paid for. Though secured by Christ's cross and resurrection, our resurrection bodies come to us, according to the New Testament, only when Christ returns. And the same *may* be true, in many instances, of healing. God *may* bestow healing now, but He has certainly not pledged Himself to do so. But one day, all true believers will be perfectly healed.

And *third*, this means that if Jesus' healing miracles during the days of His ministry are to be seen as a fulfillment of Isaiah 53, it is because that healing ministry was itself a function of the death and resurrection that would follow. If Jesus' healings had not been followed by His sacrificial death and victorious rise from the dead, they would have been mere displays of power— but they would not have dealt with our sin and rebellion, the underlying problem, the ultimate ground of all sickness.

Thus, even Jesus' healing miracles point to the truth set out as early as Matthew's first chapter: Jesus came to save His people from their sins (1:21). And the same tight connection, as we have seen, lies behind the healing of the paralytic (9:1-8).

The miracles reveal multiplying facets of Jesus' authority. There is power in His very person to the believing seeker (9:20-22). He can even raise the dead (9:18,19, 23-26)—a foretaste of the final resurrection. But sadly, the most amazing displays of authority—"Nothing like this has ever been seen in Israel" (9:33)—aroused animosity in some people, who foreshadowed the conflict ahead by charging Him with occultism (9:34).

Jesus' Wisdom in His Ministry

Authority is one thing, wisdom to use it well is another. That is one of the reasons why Matthew intermingles stories of Jesus' wisdom in ministry with his accounts of Jesus' miracles (8:18-22; 9:9-13; 9:14-17; 9:35-38). Four principal facets of Jesus' wisdom and strategy emerge from these four sections.

Facet number one. If a raw pagan from the streets of one of our major cities came up to us and told us he or she wanted to follow Jesus, we might well respond with delight. The new convert would soon be baptized, introduced to brothers and sisters at church, and invited to share a "testimony." But here (8:18-22) we find two brief scenes where Jesus actually repulsed such enthusiasm. In the first, He warned the volunteer that following Him closely during the days of His ministry meant homelessness. In the second, He found the offer of discipleship too conditional, even though on any understanding of the text this man's request fell within the bounds of expected filial responsibilities. But like the disciples of 5:1,2, this "disciple" was uncertain he wanted to follow Jesus *regardless* of the cost or sacrifice.

Many want to follow Jesus, but want to follow personal preferences as well. Yet the very heart of the gospel, according to Jesus, involves utterly unqualified allegiance to Him. Repentance and faith are meaningless categories if there is no turning from self-will to Christ's will, no abandonment of proud self-confidence in favor of confidence in Christ.

And thus while we are prone to inflate numbers and try to cajole people into the kingdom, Jesus Himself put up barriers. Despite enormously broad invitations (see 11:28-30), He nevertheless insisted that there is a cost to be paid (see Luke 14:25-33), and therefore no one should profess undying allegiance to Him without careful thought. "Nothing was less aimed at by our Lord than to have *followers*, unless they were genuine and sound; he is as far from desiring this as it would have been easy to attain it."[3] Here is wisdom, mingled with profound integrity.

Facet number two. In the second section (Matt. 9:9-13), Jesus called Matthew to be a follower, and found Himself invited to a party with many characters whom popular religion then—as now—would find unsavory. Because Israel was under Roman domination, many viewed tax collectors as near traitors; and some of them at least would have risked incurring ceremonial uncleanness by coming into contact with Gentile overlords. The "sinners" might simply be those who did not observe the detailed rules observed by more fastidious Pharisees; but probably they included public sinners widely regarded as beyond the pale. Perhaps the most revealing feature about the charge leveled against Jesus—and it *was* a *charge,* even though it was phrased as a question (9:11)—is that the Pharisees did not address it to Jesus directly, but put it to His disciples.

But Jesus recognized that if He had come to save sinners from their sin, He would have to get in touch with them. He did not come to be entertained by the religious pundits but to go after sinners the way a doctor goes after the sick (see 9:12—in the days before preventive medicine!). This does not of course suggest that Pharisees did not need a Saviour; for Jesus quoted Hosea 6:6: "I desire mercy, not sacrifice."

God told apostates in Hosea's day that although they continued the temple ritual they had abandoned mercy—covenant love—thereby keeping the husk and losing the kernel. Husk and kernel belong together, of course, at a certain stage of growth. Hosea was not *abolishing* the temple rites prescribed by Moses.

The same forceful language, applied to the Pharisees, suggests Jesus was actually telling them that they were aligned with the apostates of ancient Israel, losing the heart of the matter while preserving the shell—as exemplified by their attitudes to tax collectors and "sinners." Therefore Jesus' final statement in Matthew 9:13, "For I have not come to call the righteous, but sinners," was not so much an attempt to divide humanity into two mutually exclusive groups, but rather disavowed a false image of what the Messiah came to do and substituted a correct one.

Many are the people today who think they are good enough to *deserve* Jesus' approval and blessing. Such people feel that if a religiously illustrious individual like Jesus came to town they would be the sort of people He would be delighted to visit. If they go to church or give a few dollars to feed the hungry, they almost feel as if they have done God a favor. Jesus' perception of

His mission was diametrically opposed to such nonsense. If in 8:18-22 we learn the importance of unqualified discipleship, we now learn that Jesus came for sinners (compare to the first beatitude, 5:3). That means not only that we must see ourselves as Jesus sees us, but also that we therefore treat other sinners with the compassion we ourselves need.

Facet number three. In the third section (9:14-17), Jesus answered charges that His followers were not disciplined enough in the area of fasting (compare to 6:16-18). His answer had two parts. The first was an unqualified claim that He was the messianic "bridegroom" (9:15). There is a small hint of the cross here; the bridegroom would one day be taken away. But more telling is the clarity of the claim. If Jesus spoke the truth, the only appropriate response open to the Pharisees was to join Jesus' disciples.

The second part of Jesus' answer drew two quick sketches (9:16,17). The point of both is that the newness Jesus brought, including the exuberant joy His disciples were displaying, could not be contained by traditional forms of Jewish piety. This answer was both crucial and wise, for it responded to the implied criticism (9:14) by showing that a new situation in the history of God's revelation was unfolding. The Messiah's new wine could not safely be poured into the old wineskins of Jewish tradition; the kingdom was dawning, Messiah had come, and those with eyes to see the brilliance of this new step of revelation would rejoice, not fret about doubtful religious traditions already made obsolete in certain respects.

Facet number four. The last section (9:35-38) hints at the strenuousness of Jesus' exertions; but it does more. It insists that it was Jesus' profound compassion, the kind that could weep over a city (see 23:37-39), that motivated His training of the Twelve and His commissioning of their early ministry (10:1-42). To reach such great crowds, He had to delegate some of His *authority* to them (10:1). And meanwhile, the same deeply felt needs, the same compassion, drove Him to encourage His disciples to pray and ask the Lord of the harvest to send out workers into His harvest field (9:38).

In short, Jesus envisaged a mission characterized not by

mere organization, but by fervent prayer; not personal aggrandizement, but delegation; not driving motives to build a great institution, but compassion seeking out wise strategy.

Jesus' Foresight in Training Others for Mission

The principal links between the discourse in Matthew 10 and the closing views of Matthew 9 are two: *first,* the compassion of the Saviour who saw the staggering need led naturally to the commission of other workers; and *second,* the signs of rising opposition against Jesus (9:34) prompted Him to spend a considerable part of the discourse warning His followers of the kind of opposition they too could expect.

But the mission discourse of Matthew 10 (as it is often called) is part of an even broader development. Jesus Himself, as we shall see in chapter 6 of this book, expected a substantial delay before the end would come. During that period He would build His church, using in the first instance the men that He Himself had trained.

This chapter is therefore part of a *pattern* of training that culminates in the Great Commission (28:18-20). Luke records not only this trainee mission of the Twelve (Luke 9:1-6), but also another for a larger group of 70 or 72 disciples (Luke 10:1-16). All four Gospels make it clear that Jesus spent extra time in private with the Twelve, especially just before the cross.

The discourse in Matthew 10 therefore focuses on two different levels. On the one hand, there are instructions applicable only to the trainee mission immediately ahead (10:5-16). These include the prohibition against preaching to Gentiles or Samaritans (10:5,6), the "stripped down" supplies the Twelve were permitted to take (10:9,10), and the dramatic authority delegated to them (10:8).

On the other hand, the rest of the chapter (10:17-42)—although it conveys many things useful in any Christian outreach, including this first trainee mission—clearly envisages a situation *beyond* the immediate mission. These same men would one day be flogged at the command of local Jewish councils (10:17)—certainly something that did not happen until after the Resurrection. Moreover, they would be brought before pagan governors and kings as part of their witness *to the Gentiles* (10:18), even though in the *immediate* mission they were to go only to "the lost sheep of Israel (10:6). It thus seems that Jesus wanted His followers to understand their immediate, short-term mission in terms of the life-long challenge they would face, a challenge confronted by every successive generation of Christians.

It is not possible in this little work to go through the discourse in details; but four of its themes demand brief notice.

First, in contrast to a lot of sentimental religious pap, Jesus did not expect that wherever His gospel was preached there would be instant sweetness and light. Instead, He envisaged that the preaching of the gospel would in many cases actually divide families (10:34-36). This in no way justifies the young convert who puts on airs or develops sanctimonious and offensive tactics. Rather, it presupposes that human families are already evil (see also 7:11), in rebellion against God; and when some member of the family turns his or her allegiance to the Lord Jesus, there will necessarily be conflict with family members who do not take the same step.

As powerfully as the Bible defends the importance and integrity of the family and of the responsibility of children to honor their parents, Jesus nevertheless insisted that where there is a fundamental clash between the claims of family and His own claims, His own must take precedence.

Second, on a broader scale Jesus expected that His followers would face opposition, some of it savage. He had already warned would-be followers to count the cost (8:18-22); now He returned to the theme in more lurid detail. Not only would His followers be flogged (10:17) and hauled before various officials (10:18), they would face betrayal, hatred, even death (10:21,22), as He already intimated in the Sermon on the Mount (5:10-12).

This emphasis is part of a sustained New Testament perspective. Jesus elsewhere returned to the same theme (see John 15:18—16:4); and Paul insisted that "everyone who wants to live a godly life in Christ Jesus will be persecuted" (2 Tim. 3:12). Considering the entire history of Christianity, we must recognize how anomalous the experience of many Western Christians really is. Even here, however, many face small pressures from family, employment, and friends, while elsewhere brothers and sisters in Christ often face more violent opposition.

Where the church is persecuted virtually not at all, it will either be because it is so strong as to dominate the opposition (and in that case it is in danger of arrogance, abuse of power, and overweening self-confidence), or because it has become domesticated by the surrounding culture and therefore no longer presents a threat (and in that case the church's condition is even more perilous, for God Himself will judge it—since judgment begins with the family of God; see 1 Peter 4:17). What Christians must always remember is that only those who acknowledge Christ are acknowledged by Him before the Father (Matt. 10:32,33).

Third, the reason Jesus could make such immense claims and demand such unequivocal allegiance lies in a comprehensive vision of who God the Father really is. He is the final judge who will one day demand an exact moral accounting of even the most concealed things (10:26,27). Moreover, as judge He has power not only to inflict the transient beatings Christians may face during their pilgrimage, but to "destroy both body and soul in hell" (10:28). At the same time, He is the sovereign whose reign is so extensive that not even a sparrow falls to the ground apart from His decree (10:29). He can therefore be trusted even in the midst of persecution; and sometimes He will provide very special help indeed (10:18-20).

The lesson to be learned is that knowing God in a world that does not know God, though costly, is infinitely to be preferred. It is eminently more sensible to love, fear, and trust the one to whom we must give account than to pin one's hopes and allegiance on a world already under judgment. As in the final verses of the Sermon on the Mount, so here: the ultimate rationale for believing the gospel and becoming disciples of Jesus is not the desire to have a better life *now,* but the importance of living now in the light of the judgment and vindication *to come.* Without this eschatological perspective (as it is called), the claims and demands of the gospel of the kingdom make no sense at all.

And, finally, so tightly is the follower of Jesus bound up with Jesus Himself, that the world's rejection of Jesus will necessarily be transferred to Jesus' follower (10:24,25). But conversely, this means that those who accept Jesus also accept His followers. Indeed, one may go even further, and say that those who accept Jesus' followers simply because they are such are in the same measure accepting Jesus Himself (10:40-42). This reciprocity stands at the heart not only of Christian evangelism but also of Christian fellowship.

Notes
1. Mary A. Baker, "Master, the Tempest Is Raging" in *Church Service Hymns* (Winona Lake, IN: The Rodeheaver Hall-Mack Company, 1948).
2. D. A. Carson, "Matthew," *Expositors Bible Commentary*, vol. 8 (Grand Rapids: Zondervan, 1984).
3. R. Stier, *The Words of the Lord Jesus*, vol. 1 (Edinburough: T. and T. Clark, 1874).

Questions for Further Study

1. How should Christians pray for the sick?

2. What does Matthew 9:35-38 suggest that our attitude should be toward the towns and cities and communities in which we live? What does this mean we should be doing?

3. How should we apply Matthew 9:10-13 to ourselves?

4. What prohibition is found three times in Matthew 10:26-31? Why does it make sense—what is the reason behind it? In practical terms, what does it mean we should be doing?

5. What stories of persecution for righteousness' sake do you know of? What kind of "counting the cost" do Christians where you live have to engage in?

6. How should we apply Matthew 8:18-22 to our own evangelism?

Who on Earth Is this Jesus? 5

So many of the worst of human reactions stem in part from disappointed expectations. We expect to be treated well and when we are not we react with shoddy indignation and bitterness. We expect a marriage to serve as the answer to certain dreams and when it doesn't we seek divorce. We fix our hopes on a hero—political or otherwise—and when he or she turns out to be corrupt, or merely incapable of surmounting enormous obstacles, we retaliate with disdain and rejection.

Even in religion, people may approach Christ or the church with powerful, prior expectations that are fundamentally wrongheaded. When their expectations cannot be met, they too often chase after some other ephemeral vision instead of asking where the *truth* lies, or whether the fault might rest with their own expectations.

No small part of the animosity stirred up by Jesus' ministry sprang from the fact that popular conceptions of what the Messiah would be like and what the Messiah would do were far removed from what Jesus was actually like. Because of this, the Pharisees began to spread rumors that Jesus was dabbling in the black arts (see Matt. 9:34). Now the questions, doubts, and opposition began to mount, making the central question more and more urgent: Who on earth is this Jesus?

Jesus the Successor of John the Baptist

Even John the Baptist, Jesus' forerunner, entertained doubts (11:2,3). Like his great mentor before him, the prophet Elijah, John had expected one thing and discovered something else. Elijah expected revival in the wake of his dramatic and successful confrontation on Mount Carmel (see 1 Kings 17–18). But when instead he faced the wrath and death-threats of a wicked queen, he was so frustrated, disappointed, and self-pitying that he wanted to roll over and die (see 1 Kings 19).

John the Baptist preached that the one coming after him would not only baptize His people with the Holy Spirit, but would serve as stern judge to purify the nation with fiery judgment (Matt. 3:11,12). But what did he find? Yes, on the one hand this Jesus whom he had identified as the Messiah was indeed going about doing good, apparently mightily endued with the Holy Spirit and performing the tasks promised for the messianic age (see Isa. 26:19; 28:18,19; 35:5,6; 61:1). But on the other hand, this Jesus did *not* seem to be exercising any stern judgment.

It was all right to heal the sick, raise the dead, cast out demons, still storms, preach righteousness, and announce the kingdom; *but where was the judgment?* Had the corruptions and cruelties of Caesar been abruptly shut down? Had hypocritical temple leaders been banished? Had the disgusting corruptions of Herod Antipas been confronted? Why was he, John the Baptist, languishing in the stifling heat of the prison at Machaerus fortress for challenging the morals of Herod, while Jesus the alleged Messiah did nothing about this injustice? Doesn't the Old Testament promise not only blessing in the messianic age, but *justice?* Even the passages just cited from Isaiah spring from contexts that marry the two themes of blessing and judgment. The doubts multiplied, until the Baptist asked, "Are you the one who was to come, or should we expect someone else?"

Jesus' answer was in two parts. The first was addressed directly to John's disciples (Matt. 11:4-6). Here Jesus briefly recounted some of the evidence lying around on every hand—

but He phrased this recital in the language of messianic Scriptures, especially Isaiah 35:5,6; 61:1,2. Ironically, both passages promise blessing *and judgment:* "Your God will come, he will come with vengeance; with divine retribution he will come to save you" (Isa. 35:4); "The day of vengeance of our God" (Isa. 61:2). But Jesus referred only to those parts of the texts that promise blessings, and then concluded, "Blessed is the man who does not fall away on account of me" (Matt. 11:6). What did He mean?

That final blessing makes the point. Jesus assumed John the Baptist had been right—Jesus Himself truly is the Messiah. But John seemed in danger of falling away. Jesus promised blessing for those who do *not* fall away—for those who begin well and continue to persevere, despite disappointed expectations. Meanwhile, by referring to the positive evidence of His compassion, preaching, and miracles as the fulfillment of Old Testament promises, Jesus was saying that at least that much of the evidence was in, and confirmed Him to be the Messiah. Implicitly, this answer suggested that the rest of the predicted evidence must wait awhile longer.

The second part of Jesus' answer was addressed not to the messengers from John the Baptist but to the crowds. Apparently some people who had once revered John no longer knew quite what to make of him. He had seemed like such a strong and influential reformer—and now he was languishing powerless in a prison. Did some think him not strong enough to escape Herod's guards and stone walls, to perform some miracle to smash the tyranny (11:7)? Was it perhaps that they expected a powerful spokesman for God to display a little pomp and splendor (11:8)? Or did the more insightful in the crowd rightly take John to be a prophet, yet fail to see his deeper importance (11:9)?

For that is how Jesus defended John the Baptist. Yes, Jesus argued, John was a prophet, a true spokesman for God; but he was more. He was also the *subject* of prophecy; for the last canonical prophet of the old covenant had promised to send a preparatory messenger—and that messenger, Jesus affirmed, was John the Baptist (11:9,10, citing Malachi 3:1).

How did that make John more than a prophet? The answer

lies in the role of this preparatory messenger. Once that preparatory messenger had come, then "suddenly the Lord you are seeking will come to his temple" (Mal. 3:1). As Malachi said elsewhere, "See, I will send you the prophet Elijah before that great and dreadful day of the Lord comes" (4:5). Now since Jesus was claiming that John the Baptist fulfilled prophecies, and since John announced the arrival of Jesus, then Jesus must also have been saying that His *own* arrival on the scene was the fulfillment of the promise that "the Lord whom you seek" was here at last, that the "great and dreadful day of the Lord" had dawned.

This is what made John the Baptist so great: he had the privileged task of pointing out the Messiah, of preparing the way before Him. In one sense, of course, Moses, Isaiah, Jeremiah, and other prophets also pointed to the coming of Christ; but only John the Baptist personally pointed Him out. And that is what made John, in Jesus' estimation, the greatest human being ever to have been born up to that time (Matt. 11:11).

The claim was staggering. John the Baptist, according to Jesus, was greater than Julius Caesar, greater than Alexander the Great, greater than Homer or Socrates, greater than Moses or Daniel—precisely because he pointed out the identity of the Messiah in a way no one had ever done before. John the Baptist never performed any miracle (see John 10:41); but he was a true witness at a crucial point in the history of redemption. More stunning yet, it was Jesus who gave this evaluation. That means that although in one sense Jesus was justifying John's greatness to the crowds, in a deeper sense He was affirming His *own* identity as the promised Messiah, since John the Baptist announced His coming and pointed Him out.

But there is one further conclusion to be drawn from this evaluation of John the Baptist, and Jesus made it explicit: "He who is least in the kingdom of heaven is greater than he" (Matt. 11:11). The measure of this greatness must be the same as that used to gauge John. The point is clear: John was the last in a long line, the culmination of "the Prophets and the Law" that together "prophesied" the coming of Jesus and the kingdom (11:13). But now, with the actual coming of Jesus, even the least believer in the dawning kingdom is able to point Jesus out and witness His work more clearly than John the Baptist could.

So often Christians want to establish their "greatness" with reference to their work, their giving, their intelligence, their preaching, their gifts, their courage, their discernment. But Jesus unhesitatingly affirmed that even the least believer is greater than Moses or John the Baptist, simply because of his or her ability, living on this side of the coming of Jesus the Messiah, to point Him out with greater clarity and understanding than all His forerunners ever could. If we really believe this truth, it will dissipate all cheap vying for position and force us to recognize that our true significance lies in our witness to the Lord Jesus Christ.

Jesus the Revealer of the Father

There is another way of looking at John the Baptist and Jesus. One may, of course, compare their relative roles in God's purposes of redemption, as Jesus did. In that case, Jesus was the object of witness, and John was the one who bore witness to Him.

Alternatively, one might contrast their personal life-styles: John the Baptist was abstemious, a relative recluse, frugal; Jesus was happy to go to parties and was certainly prepared to take a drink (11:18,19). In this case, the contrast reveals less about the two men than about the way most people responded to them. They dismissed John as a fanatic, demon possessed; and they wrote Jesus off as a glutton and a drunkard. Such people are like whining, discontented children in the marketplace who are never satisfied with any game. But wisdom—right living before God in *both* the case of Jesus *and* of John—is proved right by her actions (see 11:19). Their respective life-styles were *both* acknowledged as the path of wisdom.

If men and women will not respond with repentance, faith, and obedience to the revelation God graciously provides, then sooner or later there must be denunciation. Jesus denounced in the strongest terms the cities where most of His miracles had been performed—Korazin, Bethsaida, Capernaum, Galilean towns greatly favored by being the places where Jesus focused

His ministry. But in fact, they had not repented, even though similar revelation would have brought Tyre and Sidon—pagan cities to the north—to their knees, and effected a change in conduct in Sodom, proverbial for wickedness (Genesis 19).

Three very important truths lie behind this forceful denunciation. *First,* it is presupposed that God does not owe salvation to anyone. Otherwise, God could be charged with injustice for withholding from Tyre, Sidon, and Sodom the further revelation that He knew would bring them to repentance and faith. But God does not look at the world as an aggregate of morally neutral human beings to whom He is pledged to give things or who must receive every incentive to salvation. Far from it. He sees the world as an aggregate of revels, of sinners, of men and women to whom He owes nothing (see Rom. 1:18–3:20). If He condemned all, His justice would not be tarnished. Yet in mercy He saves many of these rebels—even though He *owes* mercy to *none*!

Second, God has what the philosophers call "contingent knowledge." That is, He not only knows what any individual or group has done, is doing, or will do, but He also knows what they *would have done* under different circumstances; and He takes this knowledge into account at the final judgment. Sodom is in better shape for the judgment than Capernaum, not because Sodom actually obeyed God more or better than Capernaum, but because God knows that if Sodom had enjoyed all of Capernaum's advantages, Sodom would have repented and far outstripped Capernaum in moral excellence and discernment. To put it another way, at the final judgment God will take into account not only North America's and every North American's moral standing and response to Jesus Christ and use of opportunities, as compared with, say, every Cuban's use of the same—but also what both parties would have done if their roles and advantages had been reversed.

And *third,* for Jesus to say it will be "more bearable" for this group than that on the day of judgment presupposes that there are degrees of felicity in paradise and degrees of torment in hell (see 12:41; 23:13; Luke 12:47,48), a point Paul certainly understood (see Rom. 1:20-2:16). I do not know three other truths more calculated to sober us and drive us to our knees in repentance.

If the revelation of God in Christ Jesus has been so thoroughly rejected, does this mean God's purposes to save some are thwarted? Far from it. For Jesus praised His Father for hiding these things from the wise and learned, and for revealing them to little children (Matt. 11:25,26). Indeed, so closely is the revealing work of the Father linked with the revealing work of the Son, that Jesus can also say, "No one knows the Father except the Son and those to whom the Son chooses to reveal him" (11:27).

There are three things to learn from these statements. *First,* regardless of how John the Baptist may have temporarily doubted Him, and the populace at large failed to repent, Jesus saw Himself as the supreme revealer of the Father. It is not surprising that "no one knows the Son except the Father," but it is astonishing that "no one knows the Father except the Son"—and those to whom the Son reveals the Father (11:27).

A claim like that brooks no middle ground: either Jesus was the exclusive revealer of God, or He was a nut. If the former, we must bow to Him, acknowledge His lordship, receive His word of revelation, delight in His truth and in the knowledge of God only He can provide. If the latter, we must dismiss Him at once, and entertain no more pious nonsense about Jesus being one good man or one revealer among many.

Second, these statements show there is both an objective revelation and a subjective revelation. The *objective* revelation was *there,* in the person and ministry of Jesus; but that did not mean everyone *perceived* it to be there. For such perception a person must also receive *subjective* revelation—that is, a work in his or her own mind and heart that enables him or her to *recognize* who Jesus was, and thereby come to know the Father.

Third, those who enjoy this subjective revelation, those to whom the Son chooses to reveal the Father, are invariably the "children"—that is, not the wise and learned, the self-sufficient and self-important, but the meek, those who recognize their spiritual poverty (see 5:3) and hunger to be taught by God.

Many religious Jews felt that when Messiah came He would

not only end Rome's rule and establish the pre-eminence of
Israel in the college of nations, but would elevate Israel's leaders, her priests, theologians, and patriots, to positions of prestige and power. Such an outlook was not likely to stress the
emphasis on righteousness, justice, mercy, and forgiveness of
sin bound up with the Old Testament promises of Messiah's
reign.

The leaders' expectations bred their disillusionment with
Jesus; for here He was, favoring the weak, the despised, the
weary, and the burdened (11:28), and doing nothing to pulverize
the Gentiles and teach them their place. But the error of the
leaders, as we shall increasingly perceive, was not simply an
intellectual misunderstanding. From Jesus' perspective, it
involved a *moral* failure to recognize their own greatest need, to
value righteousness and justice, to yearn for the forgiveness and
wholeness only Jesus could provide.

So Jesus' generous invitation (11:28-30) is to the broken and
the burdened. It is grounded in His own gentleness and humility:
He was not simply a powerful lord who ruthlessly crushed all
opposition, but one who sought the good of others and promised
rest for their souls (11:29). The yoke He promised was not the
yoke of the law, but discipleship to Him: "Learn from me," He
said, which does not mean "imitate me" or "train from my experience" so much as "learn from the revelation that I alone
impart." And this discipleship, this yoke, is "easy" (good, comfortable—not challengeless) and His burden light.

Jesus the Lord of the Sabbath

The contrast between Jesus' "yoke" and that of others now
became clearer. It was not found in some tension between law
and grace, or between difficult and easy commandments. No,
the contrast lay between the burden of submission to the Old
Testament in terms of Pharisaic regulations and the relief of
coming under Jesus' tutelage as under the authority of the gentle
Revealer to whom the Old Testament, the ancient paths, truly
pointed.

Many Jewish authorities had developed a complex web of
rules of conduct, rules with only a tenuous link to the Old Testa-

ment itself. They established 39 separate categories of work prohibited on the Sabbath and, since reaping was one of them, they condemned Jesus' disciples for picking some heads of grain as they took a Sabbath stroll through a nearby field.

Jesus might have answered by saying that the Pharisees' rules went way beyond the Old Testament text. His disciples, after all, were not farmers whose regular employment made them work in the fields six days out of seven, and who were therefore trying to slip in a little Sabbath overtime on the sly. Their activity was casual, harmless, was staving off their hunger, and was not a return to their normal labor. But instead, Jesus' answer ran along quite different lines.

First, He noted the exception David was prepared to make to formal prescriptions of law when, desperate and hungry, he and his men ate some of the consecrated bread of the Tabernacle—bread that should only have been eaten by priests (Exod. 25:30; Lev. 24:5-9; 1 Sam. 21). The thrust is not that rules often have exceptions, but that the Pharisees' entire *approach* to the question of law was fundamentally wrong since it could not explain a story in the Scriptures themselves. Moreover, if David's authority could cover both himself and his men, there is just a hint that Jesus' authority could cover both Himself and His disciples.

Second, Jesus pointed out that not all laws operate on the same level. Formally, the priests "broke" the Sabbath laws by observing the Temple laws requiring them to work on the Sabbath (Matt. 12:5)! But the precedence of the Temple laws over the Sabbath laws shields the priests from guilt. Yet now, Jesus insisted, "One greater than the temple is here" (12:6). To any first-century Jew, this would be an astonishing claim. Jesus was saying that He Himself, or perhaps the kingdom He was even now inaugurating, was greater than the Temple! By analogy, therefore, His own authority transcends the authority of Sabbath laws.

Third, Jesus again cited Hosea 6:6 (see Matt. 12:7; also 9:13) and insisted not only on the innocence of His disciples, but argued that the reason why the accusers must stand accused of condemning the innocent was because they misunderstood the heart and thrust of their own Scriptures. The disciples were innocent simply because the Son of Man is Lord of the Sabbath: the "one greater than the temple" was here.

To the account of this Sabbath confrontation, Matthew appended another (12:9-14). Here Jesus made a further point. The rules established by Pharisees allowed them to rescue a trapped sheep on the Sabbath; so why should not Jesus do good to a man on the Sabbath, since a man is much more valuable than a sheep (12:11,12)! The miracle itself (12:13) confirmed Jesus' judgment on the matter, just as the miracle in 9:1-8 confirmed Jesus' authority to forgive sins. But so blind were His opponents that the confrontation deepened their opposition and helped to foster a conspiracy that would end in the cross (12:14).

Jesus, God's Chosen Servant

Aware of the rising plots, Jesus withdrew from that spot (12:15), even by this withdrawal showing that at this stage at least He did not feel called to crush all opposition. The irony is that the opponents whom He thus spared were the very ones who thought a proper Messiah *should* crush all opposition! Instead, Jesus continued His healing ministry, enjoining those He healed to keep silent. This silence not only helped to keep under control the expectations of the crowd that wanted to make the Messiah not much more than a miracle-worker (compare to 8:4; 9:30) but also, according to Matthew, fulfilled Scripture (12:17-21).

By contrast with the Pharisees who were plotting Jesus' death, Jesus continued His healing ministry, and discharged His role with tranquility and gentleness (12:19,20). The Scripture quoted in Matthew 12:18-21 is from Isaiah 42:1-4, one of the "suffering servant" songs. In other words, despite his consistent demonstration that Jesus is the Messiah, the royal Son of David, and unique Son of God, Matthew very carefully insisted that Jesus' person and ministry must not be interpreted *in those categories exclusively.* Rather, His person and ministry must *also* be interpreted as fulfilling Old Testament prophecies about the coming suffering servant.

The Scripture quoted conveys many delightful sketches of

Jesus the suffering servant. For example, He is presented as the one whom God chooses and loves, calling to mind the voice at Jesus' baptist (3:17) and transfiguration (17:5). He is the one on whom God pours out His Spirit—indeed, without limit (John 3:34)—enabling Him to proclaim justice to the nations.

Two favorite themes of Matthew thus reappear. First, the God of the Bible and His Son Jesus Christ are interested in *justice,* righteousness both personal and social, holiness, purity. Second, Jesus' proclamation is not for Jews only but also for the nations. At the very time many Jews felt Jesus was insufficiently nationalistic, Jesus Himself was beginning to fulfill a prophecy that insisted, "In his name the nations will put their hope" (Matt. 12:21).

In due course, Jesus would predict His own return, His firm rule, the final judgment over which He will preside (see 13:40-43; 24:30,31,36-41; 25:31-46). But at this stage of His ministry He fulfilled the passages of Scripture that spoke of His gentleness. The servant of the Lord would not "quarrel or cry out" (12:19): if confronted, He would be prepared to withdraw (12:15; see also 4:12; 14:13; 15:21; 16:4). While stampeding zealots and other "strong" types thoughtlessly snapped off reed stems that were already bruised, or snuffed out a lamp wick that was merely flickering, Jesus the suffering servant bound up the bruised and fanned the feeble flame to life (12:20). His ministry of meekness and compassion refused to trample on the weak. Others might argue that the end justifies the means; but He persisted in this policy "till he leads justice to victory" (12:20).

Who is this Jesus? He is not only the royal Son of David, the unique Son of God, but also the meek and compassionate suffering servant.

Jesus, the One Who Binds Satan

There had already been some muttered speculation that Jesus' exorcisms only proved He was in league with the devil (9:34). Now those charges broke out into the open. What set them off was a combination of two factors: some further dramatic displays of Jesus' authority to cast out demons (12:22) and the provocative wonder of the people that made them ask if

Jesus might be the promised Messiah, the Son of David (12:23). That was enough to make the Pharisees fear they were losing their hold on the people; and so they again leveled their infamous accusation (12:24).

The accusation touched off three important lessons. *First,* by several analogies, Jesus made it clear that His persistent destruction of Satan's forces could not possibly be the work of Satan (12:25-29). But in a context where Jesus' claims were messianic, that left only one alternative: "But if I drive out demons by the Spirit of God, then the kingdom of God has come upon you" (12:28). Notice: "the kingdom *has come* upon you," not simply *will come.* (See discussion in chapter 2 of this book).

Second, if the kingdom had in some sense already come, neutrality with respect to Jesus was a sign of moral failure—the failure to recognize what should have been obvious for anyone with eyes to see. Therefore neutrality of this sort is tantamount to opposition (12:30). Still worse is the "blasphemy against the Spirit" (12:31,32)—the willful assigning of what is unambiguously the Spirit's work in the ministry of Jesus (12:28) to the devil (12:24), the self-conscious and malignant disputing of the indisputable. For this sin there cannot be any forgiveness, "either in this age or in the age to come" (12:32). This was the sober verdict of the only person who has the authority on earth to forgive sins (9:6).

And *third,* it follows that the fundamental problem in those who failed to recognize who Jesus was or who actively opposed Him, lay *in themselves.* They were like bad trees which inevitably produce bad fruit. Just so: every word they spoke, not least in the snap assessments of Jesus, revealed the heart's overflow (12:34). We will one day have to give an account not only of our major triumphs, but even of every insignificant word we have ever spoken (that is what "careless" in 12:36 means), for such words betray what gushes forth from our hearts, what we truly are.

That is the supreme irony. So confident was Jesus of His own role that when people ask, "Could this be the Son of David?" (12:23), or utter blasphemies (12:24), it is not He who is being assessed, but they.

Jesus' Sign

Still trying to come to grips with who Jesus was, but unable and unwilling to bend their own presuppositions to the revelation Jesus brought, the Pharisees and teachers of the law asked Him to present some authenticating miraculous sign (12:38). In one sense, of course, they were within their rights as leaders of the people to challenge the claims of all messianic pretenders. But Jesus saw their problem was in this case far deeper. After all, He had performed scores, perhaps hundreds, of miraculous signs, each one attesting to the spectacular inbreaking of the kingdom's power. Clearly, what they wanted was something different. They were demanding a miraculous sign performed *on demand,* a sort of showpiece attestation. But that would have been a domestication of God's saving reign. It would have signified a use of God's power in subservience to the ruling authorities. The power of the kingdom was not available for whimsical display and Jesus was not a trained seal, happy to do tricks on cue. In that sense, therefore, no sign would be given to a generation sunk in spiritual adultery (12:39).

But in another sense, a single exception might be made. It was not an exception in one sense: the sign Jesus offered could not be domesticated at all. But it was nonetheless important. The "sign of Jonah" was that *Jonah was.* The Ninevites of Jonah's day learned what had happened to Jonah and how he had come to their city. *He himself* was a sign by his miraculous escape from death. So also Jesus the Son of Man, after a similar period of time, would escape the chains of death. The resurrection of Jesus Christ would be sign enough (12:40).

But there is a second point of comparison between Jonah and Jesus. Both preached repentance. Yet here comparison slides into contrast; for Jonah's hearers repented, and Jesus' hearers, by and large, did not, even though Jesus outstripped Jonah, Solomon, or any other Old Testament prophet. As in 11:20-24, therefore, the generation that had turned its back on so much light stood in danger of the most severe judgment. Neutrality toward Jesus, especially on the part of those who have received the most benefit, is extremely dangerous (12:43-45).

Conclusion

Who then is this Jesus?

False expectations are subtle things. Even Jesus' immediate family apparently expected a certain intimacy with Him that His sense of messianic calling reserved exclusively for His disciples (12:46-50).

Ultimately, if we are to worship the Lord Jesus Christ who actually exists, bowing to His Lordship and experiencing His forgiveness and grace, we must be prepared to come to terms with all the revelation of Jesus recorded in Scripture, and seek to make sense of the whole. If we pick and choose only those parts we prefer, we may, like many of the Pharisees in Jesus' day, be pursuing a "Christ" who does not exist. We may even be disappointed by the *real* Christ, if we first concoct a distorted mental image of what He must be like. In no area of Christianity is it more important to seek a truly biblical balance and proportion.

Questions for Further Study

1. What establishes your greatness before God?

2. How does your town or city compare with Bethsaida and Sodom, in terms of its treatment of the light of revelation and its danger at the judgment?

3. How would you characterize the person who comes to Jesus, according to 11:25-30?

4. Is Sunday the Christian Sabbath? (This question should be attempted only on the basis of more extensive biblical study.)

5. What implications does 12:18-21 have for styles of Christian leadership today?

6. What kinds of "insignificant" things do we say that reveal the kind of people we really are?

7. Are you a "relative" of Jesus in the terms of 12:48-50?

8. Summarize who Jesus is on the basis of your study of Matthew 11—12.

Parables of the Kingdom 6

Everyone likes a good story. A few people like poetry, a few others love technical studies, and still others delight in abstract thought and advanced philosophy. But everyone likes a good story.

Some stories are told primarily to entertain; but even these convey something besides the plot—a world view, perhaps, or a moral, a profound insight into common behavior. A carefully crafted story can be an ideal way to get behind someone's defenses when a merely abstract argument could be easily parried in the cut and thrust of debate.

Many parables Jesus told were a certain kind of story. The word "parable" itself can cover an immense range of literature: it can, among other things, refer to a proverb (Luke 4:23), a nonverbal symbol or image (Heb. 9:9), a profound or obscure saying (Matt. 13:35), some kind of comparison without the trappings of plot (Matt. 15:15), and much more.

But here we are interested in parables that tell a story. Such a story is in fact a kind of extended metaphor. All the elements in the story fit the story itself; but the story as a whole, and sometimes some of its parts, shed light on something outside the story, because that "something" is usually said to be *like* what takes place in the story. And if the story has a surprise ending, it can very quickly impart large new horizons of understanding to the reader or hearer!

There are eight parables in Matthew 13. The first four appear to have been delivered in a public place before large crowds (13:1,2), and the last four to Jesus' disciples in the privacy of a house (13:36); but all *explanations* of parables were given solely to His disciples (13:10-23). Many interesting facets emerge from careful study of how the parables are grouped, arranged, and ordered; but I shall leave such considerations to the commentaries, and focus on what each parable means, concluding with some mention of the explanation Jesus gives as to why He spoke in parables. Above all it must be remembered that by outlining what a parable-story *means,* instead of telling a story myself, in one sense I am losing something; for the story form has a peculiar compulsion not easily transferred to other forms.

The Parable of the Soils

The basic ingredients in the first story (13:3-9) would be largely familiar to any Jew living in the land during the first century. The farmer goes out to sow his seed, sprinkling it on the ground with his hand as he scoops it out of a pouch tied to his waist. The seed lands in a variety of places. Paths of hard, trodden dirt crisscross his field and the seed that lands there, unable to penetrate the soil, is soon pecked away by the birds. Some falls on "rocky places"—places where the limestone bedrock is not far from the surface. Since the soil is so shallow here, it warms up quickly in the spring sun and the seeds germinate and sprout in a promising way. But when the sowing season ends and the blistering sun pelts the plants relentlessly, their roots are impeded by the bedrock and can find no water. These most promising of plants wither and die without ever bearing fruit. Still other seeds begin to produce but find life choked out by heartier thorns. But some seed falls on good ground and produces abundant crop in varying degrees, depending on the soil.

The interpretation of the parable is provided by Jesus in Matthew 13:18-23. Not every detail is given some interpretation outside the story itself; no explanation is offered for the sower, the rocky soil, the path, or the diverse yield. Yet once the main point of the story is clear, a number of the details in the story reinforce and clarify it by having non-metaphorical counterparts.

The general point is that whenever "the message about the kingdom" (13:19) is proclaimed, it receives varied reception. Some people are so hard that the message never penetrates. Others are so shallow that although they respond joyfully the Kingdom message never really takes root in their life. At the first whiff of opposition they disavow their allegiance as quickly and as thoughtlessly as they once professed it. Still others receive the message, but competing interests and concerns choke it to death.

All these "soils," these would-be converts, these professions of faith, ultimately prove fruitless; but they tell us just how intimately involved with the message about the Kingdom a person may be, while still falling short of sustained life and fruitfulness. The fourth-century preacher John Chrysostom remarked, "Mark this, I pray thee, that the way of destruction is not one only, but there are differing ones, and wide apart from one another. Let us not soothe ourselves upon our perishing in all these ways, but let it be our grief in whichever way we are perishing."[1]

But some seed falls on good, receptive ground, eventually producing fruit in various yields; these people hear the word and understand it. Although the degree of fruitfulness differs from person to person, even the least productive soil, provided there is some production, is called "good."

There is a further implication in this parable that would have been far more startling when Jesus first told it, and helps to explain why even the disciples did not understand the parable until Jesus took them aside and unpacked it for them. We saw in the last chapter that many Jews expected the Kingdom to be imposed firmly, even ruthlessly, and suddenly. But here is a story whose plot line requires *time*. In this account of the Kingdom's advance, a great deal turns on the receptivity of the people to whom the message is preached.

Just as Christians today believe that when Jesus comes again there will be no more opportunity for evasion, opposition, delay, or degrees of receptivity, so many first-century Jews believed that when the Messiah came the end was at hand. Small wonder that the first people to hear this parable found it hard to understand just what Jesus was driving at!

The Parable of the Weeds

In this second parable (13:24-30), this question of the delay of judgment becomes even stronger.

Here the Kingdom of heaven is likened to the story about a man who sows good seed in his field. But while he and his workers are sleeping (and no moral blame is attached to this sleeping, which implies only that the enemy was stealthy, not that the servants were irresponsible), an enemy comes and sows weeds among the wheat. The word for weeds probably refers to bearded darnel, difficult to distinguish from wheat when the plants are young. Even the roots of the two plants entangle themselves together.

Eventually the owner's servants spot the weeds as the plants mature and become readily distinguishable; and the owner rightly puts his finger on the source of the problem—some unnamed "enemy" (13:28). The point of the story now becomes clear in the conflict between the servants' recommendation (13:28) and the owner's decision (13:29,30). They want to rush in and attempt a separation between wheat and weed on the spot; but he decides to delay until the harvest, when the two kinds of plants are easily distinguished and can be separated and sent to quite separate destinies.

Again Jesus provided the interpretation of His own parable (13:36-43); and again it is important to observe in passing how many features in the story are not given any nonsymbolic equivalent (for example, the fact that the wheat is sown before the tares but the tares are gathered first; the conversation between the owner and his servants; the sleeping). But granted the main point, some equivalencies are established: the sower is the Son of Man, the good seed stands for the sons of the kingdom, the weeds represent the sons of the devil, the enemy is the devil himself, the harvest is the end of the age, and the harvesters are angels (13:37-39).

The point is stunningly clear. First-century Judaism was used to waiting for the Messiah, used to waiting for the end of the age, used to waiting for the coming of the Kingdom. But when it came, it was commonly argued, that would be it; the final judgment would take place, moral ambiguities and the seemingly endless tension between good and evil would be over.

Not so, said Jesus. The Kingdom of heaven, rather, is like *this* story. The kingdom comes, but the judgment is yet delayed. When the judgment does come, the separation is absolute, and the destinies of the sons of the Kingdom and the sons of the devil are entirely distinct (13:40-43). But, for the moment, the kingdom dawns without the judgment taking place.

Many have understood this parable to be saying that until the end of the age there will be a mixture of true and false believers *in the church*. This interpretation, however popular, will not do. Jesus says the "field is the world" (13:38) not the church. Above all, "kingdom" and "church" are quite separate categories. "Church" refers to Messiah's *people*; "kingdom" refers to God's (or Messiah's) *reign*. And this is a parable to explain what the *kingdom* is like (13:24), not the church.

Some have argued that a parable about good and evil in the world would be trite; but the problem of good and evil intermingled in the church is important and realistic. However, this is not a parable simply about the intermingling of good and evil, whether in world or church. Rather, it is a parable about how there is still a mingling of good and evil *even after the Kingdom has come;* for the judgment comes only later. Superficially, if the church were in view, why should Jesus later encourage church discipline and the attempt, at least, to maintain a relatively pure church (Matt. 18)?

The Parables of the Mustard Seed and the Yeast

These are the last two parables in this chapter (13:31-35) that are presented to the crowds.

In the first, the kingdom of heaven is likened to a mustard seed (13:31-32). More precisely, because of the formula used, it is clear that the kingdom is likened not to a seed *per se* but to *the story of* "a seed, which a man took and planted in his field" and so forth. The comparison is not with a static seed, but with a seed that undergoes certain change.

The mustard seed was proverbial for its smallness but this tiny seed produced "the largest of the garden plants," a mustard tree about twelve feet tall, big enough for birds to perch and nest in. Some might recall Old Testament passages that picture the coming Kingdom as a large tree with birds flocking to it (see Judg. 9:15; Ezek. 17:22-24; 31:3-14; Dan. 4:7-23). But if the *greatness* of the Kingdom is all that is in view, why did Jesus choose a tree that only grows a dozen feet high?

The point of the parable becomes clear if we remember to read it as a whole. No pious first-century Jew doubted that the Kingdom would come and that it would be great and glorious. Jesus was not simply reinforcing old convictions; He was teaching something new. He was insisting on the organic connection between the tiniest seed and the great climax, between the Kingdom's tiny beginning under His ministry and its glorious consummation at some future point. The small beginnings are therefore not to be despised, just as the tiny seed is not to be despised because it is not yet a tree. Once again false expectation was being exploded. The Kingdom would not come in its full splendor at the (first) coming of the Messiah.

The parable of the yeast (Matt. 13:33) makes a somewhat similar point. As the yeast produces an effect incredibly greater than its relative smallness might have suggested, so also the Kingdom. If there is a difference between this parable and the last one, however, it is that the mustard seed suggests extensive growth whereas the yeast suggests intensive transformation.

Another small point has been wisely noticed by a French scholar, Jacques Dupont. In both of these two short parables, the comparison Jesus chose was at first glance rather bizarre—the mustard seed because, as we have seen, the resulting tree is not as large as might be hoped and the yeast because it was commonly used as a symbol for evil (though not always, see Lev. 7:13; 23:15-18). But that is precisely the point. Jesus chose strange comparisons on occasion to evoke surprise and thought, thereby encouraging people to penetrate the parable's meaning.

The Parables of the Hidden Treasure and the Pearl

These two parables (13:44-46) do not so much deal with the hidden form of the kingdom and the delay before its consummation as with the kingdom's superlative worth. Even so, it is presupposed that the kingdom that is worth so much is in some sense hidden and waiting to be found or bought. The final, consummated form of the kingdom can certainly not be pursued this way; for when it comes at the end of the age, it comes spectacularly, by an act of God alone.

Under rabbinic law, if a workman came across a treasure in his master's field—left there perhaps by some previous generation trying to hide its wealth from successive hordes of invaders—he had two choices. If he lifted it out, it became the property of his master; but if he left it where it was, he could quite legally wait until he accumulated enough money to buy the field, and only then remove the treasure.

The parable of the hidden treasure (13:44) does not assess the morality of this distinction, any more than the parable that compares Jesus' second coming with the break-in of a nighttime thief charges Jesus with surreptitious entry or malice. The point of the comparison with the thief is that Jesus' return will be a surprise, like a thief's visit; and the point of this parable is the supreme value of the "treasure," the Kingdom of heaven, which is worth every sacrifice. Whatever the cost of the field, the treasure is worth far more; whatever the cost in discipleship, the Kingdom is worth far more. Those who come to understand just where this treasure lies will cheerfully abandon everything else in order to possess it.

The parable of the pearl (13:45) is not designed to show that a person can buy the kingdom, but that even a person who spends all his life on pearls will, once he has found a truly superlative pearl, cheerfully sacrifice all his other treasures to obtain it. So also the person who spends all his life on previous religious treasures will gladly exchange all for the Kingdom of heaven. Its worth far outstrips all other pretensions of wealth.

The Parable of the Net

Once again Jesus drew the elements of His parable from the events of everyday life (13:47,48). Some fishermen take a good catch using some kind of dragnet. Once beached, the net full of fish is emptied and the fish are sorted. Worthless fish—presumably those that can neither be eaten nor sold—are thrown away, and the good fish are kept. This, Jesus said, is what the Kingdom of heaven is like (13:47), in particular at the end of the age (13:49).

In this parable Jesus is not so much focusing on what the consummated Kingdom will be like, nor on what the dawning (some call it "inaugurated") Kingdom is like, but on the situation *right at the end of the age*. At that time, good and bad are still present; but a final separation takes place, "the wicked from the righteous" (13:49), with the prospect of horrible pain for the former (13:50).

The Parable of the Owner of the House

This last parable (13:52) does not liken the Kingdom of heaven to something, but compares "every teacher of the law who has been instructed about the kingdom of heaven" to something. Even this translation, unfortunately, leaves a little to be desired. The idea is not that this scribe or "teacher of the law" has been *"instructed about* the kingdom," but that he has "become *a disciple of* the kingdom." Such a person is like the owner of a house "who brings out of his storeroom new treasures as well as old."

The word for storeroom regularly stands for the heart, its wealth and cherished values. Now an ordinary scribe or teacher of the law, Jesus implied, may bring forth *old* things from his storeroom; but a teacher of the law who has become a disciple of the Kingdom brings forth both new things and old things. It is difficult not to see here some assessment of the new revelation that was being given in the person and ministry of Jesus, revelation that fulfilled and transcended the old. Only the "discipled scribe" can understand these things.

But there are also two subtle points that must be grasped. The wording is important. Jesus did not say that understanding generates discipleship but, in this case at least, that discipleship comes first. It is the teacher of the law *who has become a disciple of the Kingdom* who is able to bring out of his storeroom new and old things. This order reflects other passages in the chapter. Discipleship to Jesus distinguishes those who are given further revelation and understanding from those who are not (13:11,12). When, in the wake of Jesus' explanations and private parables the disciples claimed to understand (13:51), Jesus reminded them of this order by telling them this parable: *"Therefore* every teacher of the law . . . " (13:52).

The second point is that just as Jesus earlier compared His disciples with prophets and the righteous from past ages (5:11,12; 10:41), now He compared them with scribes. The *New International Version* thoughtfully renders this "teacher of the law" because most scribes not only studied the sacred texts of Scripture and gave rulings, but were *teachers* of Scripture.

If Jesus' followers are likened to teachers of the law who bring forth new things as well as old things from their storerooms, there is more than a suggestion that they alone are suited to the task of bringing forth these new perspectives and teachings *and passing them on to others*. This ties in well with a major theme in Matthew's Gospel. Jesus' disciples were being trained for ministry (Matt. 10) and after His resurrection, Jesus commissioned them, the ones who had become *disciples* of the kingdom, to go and *disciple* the nations, to *make disciples* of them (28:18-20).

But Why Speak in Parables?

That, after all, was the question put to Jesus by His own disciples (13:10). Part of the answer lies in the very nature of parables, discussed at the beginning of this chapter. But at least three *theological* reasons can be adduced as well.

First, God Himself makes a distinction between the disciples of Jesus and the indiscriminate crowds (13:11,12). The "secrets of the kingdom" are given (by God) to the former but not to the latter. The "secrets of the kingdom" refer to various matters about the Kingdom that have hitherto been hidden but are now revealed.

In light of all the parables in this chapter, the heart of these "secrets" is that the Kingdom which comes finally, dramatically, explosively, and publicly at the end of the age—a truth not hidden, since most Jews believed this—was in fact already entering the world in advance of the final judgment, and in a hidden fashion to work quietly in and through people.

Those to whom it is given to understand and perceive these "secrets of the kingdom" are Jesus' disciples; to the people at large it is not given. The one who already has enough light to follow Jesus as His disciple will receive more, and will come to grasp the secrets of the Kingdom as a result (13:12). But the one who does not even have the limited light necessary to take the first steps of serious discipleship to Jesus will be given no more. Worse, he or she will also lose what little he or she does have—presumably the claim to be a true child of the covenant community (see 8:11,12). Therefore the proclamation of the Kingdom must be in a veiled way and that is one reason why Jesus preached in parables.

Second, the following verses (13:13-17) recapitulate the same lesson, but do so less in terms of the way God reveals truth to some and not to others, as in terms of spiritual dullness on the part of the people. They are always hearing the word of God, but they never understand it. Indeed, they actually close their eyes to large parts of its content, for fear that if they took a really close look, it would force them to see, understand, *and repent* ("turn," 13:15) from their ways. This prospect is unattractive to them, even as it is unattractive to many people today. So the word is spoken in parables partly as a judicial sentence of doom on those who do not want to see.

There are some broader considerations that help us understand just what Jesus is saying here. The Scriptures frequently combine themes of God's sovereign choosing and humanity's personal sin (see Gen. 50:19,20; Judg. 14:4; Isa. 10:5-7; Hag. 1:12-14; John 11:49-52). The two themes are not opposites, but complementary ways of looking at things.

This is especially important to Matthew's themes. Increasingly as his book progresses, Matthew showed that the failure of the people to understand who Jesus was and how the kingdom was dawning was simultaneously the fulfillment of prophecy (13:14) and therefore fixed in the purposes of God, while also the result of terrible rebellion against God (compare to 11:25-30 for a similar pairing of these themes). Thus, the large scale rejection of Jesus does not mean things are out of control and God's plans are getting hammered; for God Himself predicted this outcome and already pronounced the appropriate sentence. But this does not mean people bear no responsibility for their response to the revelation Jesus is and brings. Far from it. They are held deeply accountable, precisely because the revelation is so great (compare to 11:20-24).

It is this *combination* of perspectives that helps to explain the parables. It is naive to think Jesus told parables to make the truth easier to understand. In part at least it was to mask the truth. But it is also naive to think Jesus preached in parables for no other reason than to hide the truth from outsiders. If that was all He wanted to do, why not simply refrain from preaching to them at all? And why did He also use parables with His own disciples?

The truth is that His very purpose in coming was to reach outsiders and make them His disciples (see 9:35-38; 10:1-10; 28:16-20). But, to use His own words, He was wise not to cast His pearls before pigs (7:6). And so He often preached in parables; that is, in a veiled way that hardened and rejected those who were hard and rebellious, yet in a way that enlightened (sometimes with further explanation provided) His disciples, those who were beginning to see the truth. Jesus' parables do not simply carry information; rather, they exercise a discriminating function. They do not convey esoteric content only the initiated can fathom but present the claims of the inaugurated Kingdom and the prospects of its apocalyptic culmination in such a way that its implications are spelled out for those in the audience with eyes to see.

It now becomes clear why the first parable, the parable of the soils, is so important. It not only *describes* the measured advance of the Kingdom in terms of varied human responses, but *implicitly challenges the hearer or reader to ask what kind of soil he or she is.* Those who produce no fruit because they are shallow, easily distracted by wealth, or for any other reason, probably will not understand it; so it is their sentence of doom. In fact, it condemns them even if they do understand it intellectually, but refuse to accept what it reveals of the Kingdom. Eventually, they simply take offense at Him, partly because they are not willing to consider His claims (13:57). Conversely, those who bear fruit will see themselves in it, but equally they will grasp the subtle way in which the kingdom invades human society at the present time.

Third, Matthew also insists that one reason why Jesus spoke in parables was that by doing so He was fulfilling Scripture (13:34,35; citing Ps. 78:2). Precisely how He did so cannot be explored here; but it is a wonderful measure of God's control of and direction over the entire ministry of Jesus that not only His telling of parables effects God's prophesied judgment (13:14) but that even the *fact* that He preached in parables fulfilled God's purposes!

Note
1. John Chrysostom, *Homilies on St. Matthew.* Series 1, Volume 10 of *The Library of the Post-Nycene Fathers* (Grand Rapids: Wm B. Eerdmans Publishing Co., 1889).

Questions for Further Study
1. What kind of soil are you?

2. By now it should be clear that the coming to faith of the first disciples involved them in coming to understand essentially new revelation. In what ways therefore is *their* coming to faith like and unlike *our* coming to faith?

3. What does the parable of the weeds suggest about how effective the proclamation of the Kingdom will be *before* Jesus returns?

4. Why should anyone today regard the Kingdom of heaven as the supreme treasure, the pearl for which it is worth sacrificing everything?

5. List all the references in this chapter to final judgment. What kind of picture do they present?

6. What new treasures do you bring out from your storeroom?

Multiplying Ministry and Fledgling Faith

We sometimes forget that the way the first disciples came to faith is not exactly the way people come to faith today. A person who comes to genuine faith in the Lord Jesus Christ today has already come to terms with Christ's resurrection and the Holy Spirit's descent—two momentous events in the history of redemption. In taking the first steps to repentance and faith such a person must have struggled with questions about his or her own sinfulness, wrestled with whether Jesus really did rise from the dead, hesitated before the wonderful doctrine of *grace* so fully set forth in the cross. Yet, all such steps are necessarily different from the steps taken by would-be disciples *before* the cross, *before* the Resurrection, and *before* Pentecost.

Therefore when we talk about the fledgling faith of the first disciples, we must remember that their baby faith was not exactly like the baby faith of new Christians today. Modern baby faith is fledgling in that it is still immature, untested, not very well informed, young; but the baby faith of Jesus' disciples during the days of His multiplying ministry was also hindered by their inability to perceive what kind of Messiah Jesus would be. To grow really robust and strong, *not only* did their faith need testing, time, encouragement, information, and the other sorts of things that strengthen our faith today—*but also* it needed the greatest events in the history of salvation *to happen!*

That is why the stories about faith and unbelief in the Gospels can never rightly be applied to us today in a careless, thoughtless, or superficial fashion. There are, of course, many important things to learn from these accounts, but on the whole they shed more light on the nature of Jesus' messiahship than on problems of coming to faith. Their first concern is to focus attention on Jesus, not to establish a psychological profile of people who come to faith in any age. And that, of course, is just as it should be.

Point and Counterpoint

Sometimes a novelist or an historian highlights terribly important points by juxtaposing extremes: a death scene on a war front might be followed by an account of the arms merchant living in luxury, which is followed in turn by the heroic sacrifice of some unsung widow, and so forth. Music and painting occasionally use the same technique; for self-conscious contrasts sometimes help us to see depths and relationships that might otherwise be missed.

So it is in these chapters. Matthew began by relating the grisly account of the death of John the Baptist. As the Baptist was prefigured by Elijah, so his bitterest foe was a weak and wicked king manipulated by a strong and wicked wife; Herod and Herodias are the fitting counterparts of Ahab and Jezebel. The story of how John died explains Herod's soiled and superstitious conscience (Matt. 14:1,2). Next to this record of a banquet of plenty that turned into a savage execution, Matthew juxtaposed Jesus' compassion on the sick and hungry (14:13-21). In this case their manifest need resulted in supernatural provision, enough and to spare.

In the next section, Jesus' miraculous walking on the water was met first with fear (14:26) and then doubt (14:31); yet His powerful healing ministry continued unabated (14:35,36). This marvelous work, far from engendering gratitude among the religious leaders, evoked carping criticism based on a theological tradition that effectively muzzled the radical demands of the Scriptures (15:1-20). And even Jesus' disciples needed to have elementary truths explained to them (15:15,16)!

Yet ironically, even though Jesus was sent in the first instance "only to the lost sheep of Israel," He found greater faith in a Gentile woman (15:24,28). And it is the feeding of the four thousand *Gentiles* on the east side of Galilee that resulted in spontaneous praise for "the God of Israel" (15:31). Meanwhile, the Pharisees and Sadducees, pre-eminent *Jewish* leaders, were still more interested in domesticating Jesus' miracles (16:1-4; see also 12:38-45) than in discerning what they might have meant. And even the disciples, true to their limited understanding and faith, seemed painfully slow (16:5-12).

Point, counterpoint. The drama moves on, each contrast making Jesus stand out more and more clearly, and leading already to the supreme confrontation that must result in the cross.

Although the contrasts are themselves important, we also need to see the individual themes more clearly. We shall focus first on Jesus' multiplying ministry, then on the disciples' fledgling faith, and then see how the two come together in the sustained flow of the last half of Matthew 16 (vv. 13-28).

Multiplying Ministry

Superficially, these chapters offer, so far as Jesus' ministry is concerned, more of the same: there is more healing (14:14; 15:30,31), more confrontation (15:1-20; 16:1-4), more teaching, especially to the disciples. There is also one brief mention of Jesus' private prayer life (14:23)—something Luke emphasized much more than Matthew. And still there are the crowds. None of these elements is unimportant, for each shows the intensity of Jesus' ministry, the extent to which He became known and was heard in His own land and among His own people.

But beyond these features, several other elements in these chapters testify to the way Jesus' ministry developed and multiplied at this stage. *First*, there are the two feeding miracles (14:13-21; 15:29-39). These demonstrate as clearly as His healings, but in a fresh way, Jesus' concern for the whole person;

and therefore they serve as a foretaste of the messianic banquet (8:11) when all of Messiah's people will experience plenty and never know want again. Moreover, like the walk on the water that followed the first feeding miracle, they belong to a small group of nature miracles—spectacular displays of messianic power that demonstrate Jesus' authority over the world of nature.

Second, there is the extension of Jesus' ministry to Gentiles. In one sense, of course, this is nothing new. We have already noticed how passages like 8:5-13 carry on the theme of Gentile inclusion traced even earlier (1:1; 2:1-12; 3:9; 4:15,16).

But in 8:5-13, for instance, the centurion whom Jesus commended was living in Jewish territory, and was in some measure sympathetic to the Jewish religion. The healing of the Canaanite woman (15:21-28) is rather different. It took place *outside* Jewish territory. Moreover although Jesus repulsed her request for aid when she addressed Him as Son of David—after all, she was addressing Him as if she herself belonged to the old covenant people—her ready acceptance of the Lord's response, her simple cry for help, and her understanding that Gentiles had to be fed only after the children of Israel had first been given their spiritual food (15:25-27) all combined to win the healing she was seeking.

Matthew's inclusion of the second feeding miracle is no less significant for it suggests he very carefully decided to include a Gentile feeding (which the second was) to match the feeding of Jews. Even the difference in the number of baskets of surplus scraps may draw the reader's attention to the same point. In a book that stresses 12 disciples (10:1), 12 tribes, and 12 thrones (19:28), the 12 baskets of 14:20 suggest that Messiah's supply is so lavish that even the scraps of His provision are enough to meet the needs of the covenant people.

The seven baskets of 15:37 suggests something similar; but now the 12, which inevitably calls to mind the Jewish people, is replaced by seven, suggesting fullness or completeness. Messiah's bountiful supply is so lavish that even the overflow of His provision is enough to satisfy the needs of all people everywhere.

And *third,* Jesus continued to display extraordinary wisdom in His teaching, in His confrontations with His opponents, and in His training of the Twelve. This culminated in Peter's confession (16:13-20) and in Jesus' first unambiguous mention of His impending sacrificial death and its significance for those who follow Him (16:21-28). This was a dramatic step in Jesus' ministry. We shall look at it more closely after pausing to think for a moment about how the disciples' faith was faring.

Fledgling Faith

Throughout this period of Jesus' ministry both the disciples' understanding and their faith were mixed. This was due in part, as we have seen, to the place they occupied in God's unfolding plan of redemption. But if it had not been for the sin and prejudice and traditionalism that binds all of us, they would have understood and believed much more. In other words, although their place in the stream of history made understanding and faith more difficult for them than for us, this does not absolve them from all responsibility.

Certainly that was Jesus' estimate. Consider for instance His estimate of what they should have learned from the two feeding miracles. After the first, the disciples set out to cross Lake Galilee and were threatened by a severe storm. Jesus came to them, walking on the water. After the initial shock, Peter secured Jesus' invitation to join him. But Peter's faith, strong enough to get him out of the boat and onto the water, was not strong enough to face up to the storm. Jesus saved him—and rebuked him for his doubt (14:30,31). The presupposition seems to be that if Peter had witnessed two nature miracles—the feeding of the five thousand and Jesus' walk on the water—why should he suddenly be seized with fear at this point?

More stunning yet, even after the second feeding miracle, Jesus found it necessary to rebuke the entire group of disciples. We are told that the disciples forgot to take some bread with them on one of their trips across the lake (16:5). But it happened that on this occasion Jesus, still thinking of the hardness of heart of the religious leaders (16:1-4), warned His men to "Be on your guard against the yeast of the Pharisees and Sadducees"

(16:6)—meaning, of course, their teaching which in its treatment of Jesus was permeating and influencing the nation as yeast permeates and influences bread.

But the disciples tied in Jesus' warning with their own forgetfulness—their failure to bring food—and concluded that Jesus must have been giving this obscure rebuke "because we didn't bring any bread" (16:7). This was what earned Jesus' real rebuke: "You of little faith, why are you talking among yourselves about having no bread? Do you still not understand? *Don't you remember the five loaves for the five thousand, and how many basketfuls you gathered? Or the seven loaves for the four thousand, and how many basketfuls you gathered? . . .* But be on your guard against the yeast of the Pharisees and Sadducees" (16:9-11, italics added).

In short, Jesus told them off for their little faith and their inadequate understanding, not on the basis of what they should have *anticipated* of *future* events like the cross and the resurrection, but of what they should have *already* understood from the two feeding miracles. If they had truly known what spectacular displays of power He was demonstrating in those miracles, how could they seriously think He would be terribly upset because they had forgotten a little bread? Could not the one who fed many thousands manage to feed a dozen? And should they not trust His goodness toward them, having seen it so lavishly poured out on others?

This spiritual dullness was characteristic of the disciples at this point, as even Jesus suggested at one point in these chapters (15:16). This is not to say they had no faith at all, no understanding whatsoever, but that what they had was partial, immature, and mingled with a certain amount of stubborn self-will. At no point did the essentially *fledgling* nature of their faith surface more clearly than in the last half of chapter 16.

Peter, the Messiah, and the Cross

Remarkably, Jesus chose the *Gentile* area of Caesarea Philippi (16:13) to elicit from His closest disciples some estimate of who He really was. Opinion about who "the Son of Man is" (one of Jesus' favorite self-designations, a fairly ambiguous title that could be filled with more specific content in a variety of contexts) was divided (16:14). Some suggested He was John the Baptist risen from the dead (Herod Antipas, for example, 14:2). Others wondered if He was Jeremiah or some other prophet. Perhaps Jeremiah was specifically mentioned because some onlookers felt that they detected in Jesus something of the mixture of authority and suffering that characterized Jeremiah's ministry. Messianic expectations among the people were sufficiently diverse that some expected a whole series of prophets to appear before the Messiah Himself arrived on the scene.

But in answering Jesus' question the disciples apparently could not think of a voice in the nation that held that Jesus was the Messiah. John the Baptist, Jeremiah, one of the prophets— yes; but no group was prepared to proclaim Him Messiah. A few gladly assigned Him messianic titles (9:27; 15:22) but partly out of earnest flattery that wanted to gain healing or some other blessing. Doubtless many people nurtured hidden hopes that Jesus might turn out to be the Messiah. But so little did He match up to customary messianic expectations that there was still no wide-scale acknowledgement of His messianic status— none, at least, that had reached the disciples' ears.

Jesus changed the focus of His question, and asked what *His own disciples* thought of Him (the "you" is plural, 16:15). Peter answered, "You are the Christ, the Son of the living God" (16:16). This confession was so unambiguous that it marked a turning-point in Jesus' relationship with His closest followers. From here on, more truth was explained to them in private; and even if they did not understand it all, they were being accorded the information that would one day make sense of all Jesus said and did.

Certainly Jesus recognized that this was a new step in understanding, and that it sprung from the Father's disclosure of this insight to Peter (16:17). But we must be careful to avoid two opposing views.

First, we must not think that up to this moment the disciples, including Peter, entertained no hope or intuition that Jesus was the Messiah; for if that were the case, the early transfer of allegiance some of them made from John the Baptist to Jesus

(John 1:29-51) would be very implausible, and the disciples themselves extraordinarily obtuse (in light of Matthew 7:21-23; 11:2-6).

Second, we must not think that after this confession the disciples' grasp of Jesus' identity was stable and mature. Verses that immediately ensue (16:21-23) overturn so easy a conclusion. Even while getting this grand confession, Peter had no grasp whatsoever of a Messiah who must suffer and die.

So it appears, therefore, that Peter's faith was still *fledgling.* He and the other disciples were certainly ahead of the crowds in their comprehension of Jesus and allegiance to Him; but their faith was not *full-fledged* faith in the sense that would prevail after Jesus' resurrection.

Peter's confession (v. 16) received not only a "blessing" from Jesus (v. 17), but also a pun. The Roman Catholic church has often interpreted 16:17-19 to make Peter the first Pope, and to establish in principle the papal office for Peter's successors. But on any fair reading of the text, we cannot help but notice that no mention is made of "pope" or of any successors to Peter; and whatever verse 19 means, it scarcely made Peter infallible (see Gal. 2:11-14).

On the other hand, some Protestants, reacting against Roman Catholic claims, have tried to argue that Jesus pointed to Peter and said, "You are Peter," then pointed to *Himself* and continued, "and on *this* rock I will build my church." Alternatively, some have suggested that "this rock" refers neither to Jesus nor to Peter, but to Peter's confession.

The debates over these verses are legion and too technical to be probed here. But in the judgment of this author, Jesus was simply using a pun to say that *Peter* is the rock on which Jesus would build His church. Of course, this is not the only use of the rock metaphor. Peter himself elsewhere called Jesus the rock (see 1 Pet. 2:5-8).

But metaphors constantly change their use. For instance, here it is Jesus who builds His church; in 1 Corinthians 3:10, Paul is the expert builder. In 1 Corinthians 3:11, Jesus is the church's foundation; in Ephesians 2:19,20 the apostles and prophets constitute the foundation, and Jesus is the "cornerstone." Here, Peter has the keys; in Revelation 1:18; 3:7, Jesus holds the keys. A metaphor must always be interpreted within its *own* context.

This does not mean that the Roman Catholic interpretation is right after all. Rather, it recognizes that the natural reading of the passage takes Peter as the rock. And judging by the first few chapters of Acts, Peter was indeed the rock upon which Jesus built His church.

The *Kingdom* and the *church* are not the same thing in precisely the same way that a hippopotamus and a space suit are not the same thing. They belong to separate categories: one is an animal, the other a very recent and synthetic piece of inorganic equipment. Similarly, the *Kingdom* is the reign of God, manifest in the person and ministry of Jesus; the *church* is a group of people, Messiah's people, redeemed by Him and sworn in allegiance to Him. But it is God's kingdom, His powerful reign, that calls the church into being; and the church, God's redeemed people, proclaims the Kingdom, lives out its life even now, and one day enters and inherits the Kingdom in its consummation.

This book is not the place to enter into lengthy discussion over verse 19, but some conclusions can be stated here and are defended at length elsewhere. In Luke 11:52 Jesus denounced certain false teachers for taking away "the key to knowledge," thereby preventing many from entering the kingdom.

If Peter, by contrast, *had* the keys to the kingdom, in all probability he had the key of knowledge to enable people to enter the kingdom, not merely some personal authority. That personal knowledge was bound up with the revelation of who Jesus was—revelation Peter had manifestly been given by the Father (Matt. 16:17). Therefore if the text says Peter had the ability to bind or loose by wielding these keys of knowledge—by proclaiming the gospel and by making decisions as to who enters and who does not enter on that basis alone—it means Peter would admit and exclude people from entering on the basis of the revelation given him. So indeed he does in the book of Acts (see Acts 2:14-39; 3:11-26; 4:11,12; 8:20-23). Indeed, Peter would discover that whatever he bound and loosed, in line with this gospel, had *already* been bound or loosed (as the tenses of the

Greek verb suggest) for the decisive truth of the gospel is always antecedent to its proclamation (compare to Acts 18:9,10).

In practical terms, this means these difficult verses have to do with who is admitted to the church, and on what basis. Men and women are not *born* into the community of Messiah's people, as some Jews thought. Rather, they must receive the same revelation Peter did—or, otherwise put, they must be given the key of knowledge. That is a fundamental basis for admission to or expulsion from the church of Jesus the Messiah. That basis is not the performance of many pious acts, but a profound grasp of who Jesus truly is. And that is why the one other passage in Matthew with close links with Matthew 16:19 talks explicitly about church discipline (Matt. 18:15-18). The church must never degenerate into a polite club of vaguely religious people who happen to be born into a so-called "Christian" country.

In one sense Peter was speaking for all the disciples; certainly all of them are told to keep quiet about their new depth of understanding (16:20). Part of the reason they needed to maintain silence was that their level of understanding was still faulty, and they would have botched things badly if they had simply gone out everywhere and loudly proclaimed that Jesus was the Christ, the Messiah. That is made clear from the remaining verses in the chapter (16:21-28).

They are remarkable verses indeed. They make clear two things. *First,* although Peter had truly grasped that Jesus was the Messiah, he (and presumably the other disciples as well) was still a long way from understanding that the promised Messiah had to be not only the King, the descendant of David, but also a suffering servant who would be executed in shame. Peter found this thought so incongruous that he actually rebuked Jesus for uttering it (16:22) and thereby earned a rebuke himself (16:23), a rebuke of astonishing severity. Jesus recognized that any attempt to sidetrack Him from His mission of suffering and death had its ultimate source in the pit (compare to 4:1-11).

Second, these verses go even farther to insist not only that Jesus must die, but also that anyone who wants to be His true follower must take the same path (16:24-28). Quite clearly the verses are in some sense metaphorical; not every follower of Jesus dies by crucifixion. But the use of metaphor must not blind us to the radical and shocking nature of Jesus' demand. In Jesus' day, crucifixion was a death reserved for slaves, hardened criminals, and traitors. No Roman citizen could be crucified without the explicit sanction of Caesar. In our day, we wear gold or wood crosses as jewelry; in Jesus' day, the cross was a universally recognized sign of shame, torture, and death. Thus for Jesus to insist that His followers must carry the cross-beam to the place of execution and die this shameful death was astonishing at best, repulsive at worst.

Certainly Jesus did not mean to say that every minor disappointment we face is a "cross"—as in the frequently heard lament, "We all have our crosses to bear." He was not talking about personal disappointments, physical handicap, or some grinding difficulty, but about *death to self* (16:25-27). Then as now, some wanted a Messiah who would meet all of *their own* needs and desires; but Jesus turned out to be a Messiah who demands *shameful death to self-interest.* Self-fulfillment, even in following Jesus the Messiah, depends on self-abnegation; whereas pursuit of self-interest results only in frustration, death, and judgment when the Son of Man comes again (16:27).

It is relatively easy for Christians today to see the central place the cross occupies in God's eternal plan of redemption. But Jesus' first followers, living on the other side of Calvary, were profoundly confused by this aspect of Jesus' teaching. Conversely, if we today try to duck the implications of Jesus' words, it is all the more reprehensible, for we have far less excuse. At a time when a substantial part of evangelicalism wants a domesticated Jesus who blesses, satisfies, prospers, fills, thrills, and strengthens His followers, we need to hear again of a Jesus— the real Jesus—who insists that His genuine followers die to self-interest, deny themselves, and follow their Master in the way of the cross.

Questions for Further Study

1. What similarities and differences are there between the fledgling faith of the first disciples and the fledgling faith of immature Christians today?

2. What does it mean in your life, in practical terms, to "deny yourself" and "take up your cross"?

3. How does Acts 4:12 relate to Matthew 16:19?

4. Judging by the thrust of these chapters, what kind of "yeast" would Jesus likely warn us against today?

5. How many explicit or implicit references can you find to Gentiles in these chapters? Summarize them.

Displays of Glory and the Failures
of Messiah's People

As I write this, much of the western world is celebrating the anniversary of D-Day. In retrospect, the invasion of Europe by the assault on the beaches of Normandy spelled the beginning of the end for the Nazi regime. Yet for the generals involved in the planning and execution of the invasion, success was by no means assured. The weather might have wreaked havoc with the landing craft; the Germans might not have been tricked into thinking that the main landing assault would take place at Calais; the commanding German officer of the defense forces might not have taken the weekend off and gone back to Germany to visit his wife. In any case, to the foot-slogging GI, the first days and weeks of the invasion were not only confusing, but the outcome was uncertain. Unable to see the overall plan, certainly unaware of the ultimate outcome, he lived through a decisive turning point in history with only the most limited appreciation of what was going on.

In short, when crucial events are actually taking place, they are rarely self-explanatory. Their true significance often requires the perspective of elapsed time, and a certain framework of understanding. This is certainly true of most instances of God's great self-disclosure to humanity. Those who participate in such events certainly know that they are experiencing something momentous; but they may well be unable to detect much of that event's significance in the larger fabric of God's self-revelation in history. The Jews who fled Egypt at the Exodus knew that God was acting mightily on their behalf; but few if any grasped at the time that their redemption from Egypt would constitute the backdrop of a special covenant with Yahweh, still less than it would serve in many ways as the symbol of a greater redemption yet to come.

We have already detected something of the same phenomenon in connection with Jesus' life and ministry. But if this relative ignorance is true with respect to the great turning point of the cross, discussed in the last chapter, it is no less true of a number of discreet events in Jesus' life. The two chapters before us (Matthew 17—18) begin with Jesus' transfiguration—the moment before the cross when Jesus' true glory was most clearly revealed. Yet this spectacular display of glory was little understood by those who witnessed it (17:4,5) and in any case it served as a foil to further failures of understanding, faith, and appreciation among Messiah's people (17:14-27; 18:1,21).

Jesus Transfigured

The exact location of this event is disputed; but probably it took place on Mount Miron, 3,926 feet elevation, the highest mountain in the land and on the way from Caesarea Philippi to Capernaum (16:13; 17:24). Like Moses, Jesus displayed glory in a physical way; but whereas Moses' face shone because it reflected a little of God's glory (see Exod. 34:29,30), Jesus' face shown because He was "transfigured" before His three closest disciples. The verb is used in the New Testament to describe the way Christians are "transfigured" or "transformed" in character (see Rom. 12:2; 2 Cor. 3:18) without necessarily having shining faces! But in Jesus' case, the transformation was physical and was accomplished to permit His followers to witness something of the glory that was His before the world began (see also John 1:14; 17:5; Phil. 2:6,7) and that would be His again (2 Pet. 1:16-18; Rev. 1:16).

But that does not mean they understood what they were

seeing at the time. Indeed, the disciples had long learned to revere ancient figures like Moses and Elijah; and so to witness Jesus in *their* company was, as far as the disciples could see, something of an honor for Jesus—or, at very least, it provided the disciples with a scale by which to measure Jesus. Peter's offer to build an altar (17:4) was therefore made in good faith, but once more betrayed spectacular miscalculation and misunderstanding.

This becomes clear when we carefully think through what Moses and Elijah were doing here. While on earth, both had roles that looked to the future: Moses was the model for the prophet who would follow him (Deut. 18:18), and Elijah was the model for the forerunner of the Messiah (Mal. 4:5,6; Matt. 3:13; 11:7-10; 17:9-13). Moses introduced the Sinai covenant; Elijah sought to re-establish adherence to it. Both men experienced a vision of God's glory (Exod. 31:18; 1 Kings 19:9); both faced rather strange ends; and both suffered certain rejection along the way. It is hard not to think that in part they represent the law and the prophets (see Matt. 5:17; 7:12; 11:13).

What is most clear, however, is that Jesus outstripped them. If Moses and Elijah once witnessed God's glory, Jesus was so transfigured that He displayed it. *His* were the clothes that "became as white as the light" (17:2) and Moses and Elijah were talking *with him*. The testimony of the voice from heaven must be read against the backdrop of Peter's offer (17:4,5). When the disciples were prepared to erect *three* shelters, lumping Moses, Jesus, and Elijah together, they are firmly told: *"This* is my *Son,* whom I love . . . . Listen to *him!"* (Matt. 17:5. Compare 3:17; Deut. 18:18.) And when the terror of the disciples slowly dissipated, they saw "no one except Jesus" (17:8). Jesus was central, and in certain respects He superseded the law and the prophets, while still being linked with them.

The transfiguration was less for Jesus' sake than for the sake of His disciples. He was transfigured "before them" (17:2) and the voice spoke to them. If they did not fully understand it at the time, it was nevertheless a crucial step in Jesus' self-disclosure to them; and even though they were to maintain silence about their experience until after the Resurrection (17:9), it provided grist for the theological mill that would one day seek to explain and proclaim who Jesus is.

The question put to Jesus by the disciples (17:10) can be misunderstood. Many take it in this way: The disciples now understood that Jesus was the Messiah; but how were they to answer the view of the scribes to the effect that Elijah was to come *before* the Messiah put in an appearance? Their problem, in this view, was one of chronology. If Jesus was Messiah and Elijah must come first, who was Elijah? But Jesus had dealt with that point already (11:14). Moreover, if this was what the disciples meant by their question, it suggests that they understood the reference to the Resurrection in the preceding verse (17:9) and were asking something about mere chronology, even though Mark insisted they could not really understand what Jesus' mention of "rising from the dead" really meant (Mark 9:10).

The real thrust of the disciples' question lies deeper. If Elijah was to come first "and restore all things," they were asking, then how could Messiah be killed? If everything is restored, who would be around to try to execute Jesus? In other words, the disciples were still unable to find any framework in which the Messiah could be killed and therefore could rise from the dead. Their confusion was not *merely* chronological—*who must come first*—rather, it referred back to their fundamental inability to make sense of the combination of glory and suffering. At this stage, their witness of the transfiguration glory of Jesus had if anything confirmed them in their misapprehension.

Jesus answered that the *chronology* of the standard view was right: Elijah did indeed come first. But His followers needed to recognize two things. *First,* that John the Baptist had already fulfilled that prophecy and *second,* the Baptist's role in "restoring all things" was not absolute. After all, if the Baptist had restored literally *everything,* without exception, there would not be any need for a Messiah! The "restoration of all things" must be relative: he restored all that was necessary in preparation for Messiah's coming, and thus started the ball rolling toward the restoration of *literally* everything at the consummation. But in discharging his role, the Baptist faced opposition, and eventually lost his life; so why should it be thought strange that the Son of

Man should also suffer (17:11,12)?

The clearest manifestation of Jesus' glory had taken place in a context of misunderstanding and uncertainty (17:4,10); but the really grave failures were still to come.

The First and Second Failures

The disciples who fail in these verses (17:14-23) were (presumably) the nine who remained behind when Jesus took the inner three to the mountain when He was transfigured. Their failure to exorcise the demon from the epileptic boy was in one sense rather surprising; for Jesus had earlier granted them authority to heal and exorcise demons (10:1,8).

Yet perhaps their failure was not so strange after all, if we focus on two facts, both of which have considerable relevance to the modern church.

The first is that Matthew testified to a recurring pattern of success and failure among the disciples (see 14:16-21, 26,27,28-31; 15:16,23,33; 16:5,22; 17:4,10,11). They advance—and then they stumble. Peter confessed Jesus as the Messiah, and then told Him that His views on messiahship and suffering were wrong (16:13-23). If the failure of the disciples in this case lay in the area of faith (17:20), it was nothing new. In earlier situations the disciples' faith had already proven defective (14:26,27,31; 16:5,8).

Such failures arise in part from the disciples' peculiar position in the history of redemption; but to some extent they also reflect growth and development. Great oaks do not spring up overnight. If you want a dandelion patch, a few days will do; if you want a stand of cedars, you need decades of sun and storms and wind. Paul would later warn against appointing a recent convert to positions of leadership (see 1 Tim. 3:6). The Twelve learned from personal experience that spiritual maturity does not spring up like an overnight mushroom.

But there is a second fact that brings us to the heart of their failure. One perennial danger awaiting those who are granted some grace, power, or authority is the temptation to *domesticate* their gift. We have already seen how some of the Jewish leaders wanted to see *domesticated* signs and wonders. That is, they wanted the power of God manifest in the inbreaking Kingdom to be controllable, tamed, submissive to human leaders.

Now the disciples had fallen into the same pitfall. They had been accorded some supernatural authority (10:1-42) and had subsequently cast out demons and healed many people. When they approached this particular case, therefore, they doubtless expected quick, positive results. Indeed, if faith is nothing more than expecting to get what you ask for, then without a doubt the disciples approached this epileptic with strong faith. Yet the sad truth is that the Lord Jesus criticized their faith, or lack of it (17:20). Why?

It is surely not simply a question of *quantity* of faith. Jesus insisted that even if they had the tiniest particle of faith—faith the size of a mustard seed (proverbial for smallness)—they would have enough to move mountains. The word for "little faith" probably here suggests "poverty of faith" or the like. In other words, *little* faith, like a little grain of mustard seed, can nevertheless move mountains; but *poor* faith, like that of the disciples in their failed exorcism, is good for nothing. Only a tiny amount of genuine faith is needed; but the bankrupt, so-called "faith" they were exercising was useless. They approached the epileptic with a kind of faith that treats the authority entrusted to them like magic: all you have to do is say the right formula, push the right buttons, and out pops a miracle.

But real faith is less magic than trust, less rite than relationship. It does not so much seek to exercise power as to know, obey, love, and serve God. Within such a relationship, the supernatural authority is unexceptional; outside it, such authority quickly degenerates to the category of neat trick. Perhaps that is why Mark's version of this story records Jesus' rebuke in other terms: "This kind can come out only by prayer" (Mark 9:29). This does not mean that a certain kind of prayer was needed, a peculiar incantation; rather, it suggests that for the toughest spiritual assignments, even the authority already delegated to the disciples must be exercised in an environment of prayer. Such prayer is the result of true faith; conversely, such prayer nurtures true faith. And even a tiny amount of such faith would have sufficed in this case.

Few lessons are more needed in the modern church. There are no shortcuts to spiritual life and authority. The aim of spiritual maturity is not the acquisition of raw authority but a personal faith-relationship with the living God; and whatever authority He delegates to us ought to emerge from that walk of faith.

The second failure of the disciples recorded by these verses is more subtle. They were filled with grief at Jesus' repeated pronouncement of His impending death and resurrection (17:22,23). Grief at the prospect of Jesus' death might be commendable; but here it is almost certainly further evidence of failed understanding. After all, Jesus had spoken not only of His death *but also of His resurrection.* They heard only the first. And still their categories were defective: *either* Messiah was triumphant and victorious, an instant winner, *or* He was doomed to be defeated and die. The possibility of the latter filled them with grief; for at this point they could not conceive of a Messiah who triumphs *in* suffering, who is victorious *through* death.

How many of our disappointments and questionings of God arise out of our unbiblical thinking—out of our unwillingness or inability to assess all things within a truly biblical and spiritual framework?

The Third Failure

This one was exclusively Peter's. Thinking to defend his master against the insinuated charge that He failed to pay the temple tax levied on all Jewish males, Peter leapt to Jesus' defense—and betrayed his continued failure to see deeply into who Jesus really was (17:24,25).

Jesus told a parable to set Peter straight (17:25,26). In any absolute monarchy, taxes are levied among the people and paid into the king's treasury; but the royal family itself does not pay taxes. As Jesus said, the sons are exempt (17:26). This could only have meant that Jesus was the Son of the God of the temple in some special sense. As God's royal Son, He did not need to pay the temple tax. Peter's quick answer in defense of Jesus, rattled off so that critics would not depreciate the Master, turned out to be itself an unwitting depreciation of Him, a failure to grasp Jesus' unique status as Son.

But having insisted on the fact that He had no *obligation* to pay the temple tax, Jesus then miraculously provided the means for paying it (17:27). Not only so, he met Peter's tax obligations as well. It is almost as if Jesus gathered Peter up in His own exemption, and then in His own willingness to pay—"so that *we* may not offend them." Just as Jesus alone is Lord of the Sabbath (and by this status protects His followers from accusations of breaking the Sabbath, see 12:1-8) so also Jesus as the unique Son is exempt from paying the temple tax, and by this status covers Peter as well.

Certainly the nearby presence of two predictions of the cross and resurrection (16:21-23; 17:22,23) remind the Christian reader that it would not be long before the temple and its claims would become obsolete. The crucial meeting place between God and His covenant people would be the Lord Jesus Himself, the "one mediator between God and men" (1 Tim. 2:5). The temple might continue to exist for a few more decades; but no longer could it legitimately make the same claims it once did. And then it would be destroyed, razed by Roman troops in A.D. 70. None of this could Peter have grasped when Jesus told His brief parable; but Jesus' pregnant, symbol-laden language was bound to be unpacked later, after the Resurrection, and mined for its provocative theological richness.

The Fourth and Fifth Failures

These two questions (Matt. 18:1,21) betray minds still miles from Christian maturity. It is hard to believe that the first one— "Who is the greatest in the kingdom of heaven?" (18:1)—was prompted by theological curiosity alone! Indeed, two chapters later we find two of the disciples still jockeying for position (20:20-23) and the other ten were "indignant" (20:24) less because they thought the jockeying out of place than because they were afraid they might be bested at the game. Mark's account (Mark 9:33-37) records that the disciples were actually arguing over the question of their relative greatness, and fell into an ashamed silence when Jesus confronted them.

What is really pathetic about this failure is that it flew in the face of Jesus' earlier teaching and of His more recent announcements. Earlier on, Jesus had insisted that entrance into the kingdom begins with an acknowledgement of spiritual bankruptcy (Matt. 5:3) and that His Father hides the spiritual truths from the wise and learned while revealing them to little children (11:25). Yet here were the disciples pandering after greatness! Worse, Jesus had more recently twice told of His impending death (16:21-23; 17:22,23); but despite their initial grief the disciples quickly forgot their Master's suffering and returned to their own self-promotion. Who can deny that modern Christians, too, sometimes forget their mission, not to mention their Saviour and His sufferings, and squabble like pirates over the booty of position, honor, power, and prestige?

The fifth failure, like the third, is exclusively Peter's; but once again he reflected views prevalent among Jesus' disciples. The most prevalent view among rabbis regarding repeated sins was that a brother must be forgiven three times. On the fourth, there need be no forgiveness. So in suggesting *seven* times (18:21), Peter thought of himself as generous and big-hearted. Perhaps he felt he was really beginning to mature and appreciate Jesus' forgiving ways.

But Jesus' answer (18:22) showed how far Peter was from mature understanding. Not seven times, Jesus responded: Peter would have to be willing to forgive his brother 77 times. Jesus' point would be quite missed if some modern pedant were to read this verse and go away muttering, "Well, at least I can stop at the seventy-eighth! I can hardly wait." Seventy-seven is simply a much larger number than Peter's suggested seven. But the point of this large number is made clear by the parable that follows (as we shall see in a moment). All of Jesus' disciples had been forgiven much, much more than they would ever forgive, so their forgiveness of others would have to be enormously generous (18:23-35).

Meditation on this fifth failure will go a long way in preventing bitterness and feuding among Christians.

Patterns That Overcome Failure

The failures of Messiah's people occur again and again in

these chapters. By "Messiah's people" I do not mean the Jewish people, but *His own disciples,* of whom we Christians are heirs. Moreover, their failures stand out the more against the background of Jesus' transfiguration and solemn dignity before the prospect of His own death.

But if the failures were pathetic, they also have certain features in common. All five reflect too high a view of self and self's opinions and prerogatives, too narrow and legalistic a conception of faith, forgiveness, and relationships with God and humanity. If the disciples still needed to learn more of the nature of Jesus' mission, they also would benefit from learning new patterns of behavior. If they needed to live through Calvary and Pentecost in order to emerge on the other side as people who were truly committed to and changed by the new covenant Jesus' death would inaugurate, they also needed to have spelled out for them just what this would mean for their own conduct. And that is the sort of thing Jesus meant to get across in the fourth discourse recorded by Matthew (18:1-35).

Jesus began by demanding that those who enter the Kingdom of heaven must "change and become like little children" (18:3). The child is a model, in this context, not of innocence, faith, or purity, but of humility and unconcern for social status. Jesus assumed people are not naturally like that; they must *change* to become like little children. The result is self-humbling (18:4), not childish behavior (see also 10:16). It is to "little children" that God reveals His truth (see 11:25).

Verse 5 should be read together with verse 6; and if the flow of thought is carefully observed, the concern of these two verses is not literally "little children" but "these little ones who believe in me"—genuine believers, those who have humbled themselves and become like children. Verses 5 and 6 therefore promise blessing on the one who receives a true believer, and curse on the one who sets out to make such a person stumble in his or her faith (compare to 10:40-42). Indeed, not least the disciples themselves would have to deal radically with sin (18:8,9; see also 5:29,30), aware of the terrible "fire of hell" that awaits those who trifle with it.

Similarly, in 18:10-14 the expression "one of these little

ones" must be understood to refer to believers, true disciples of Jesus who have honestly humbled themselves. Not one of them is to be despised; for on the one hand, "their angels in heaven always see the face of my Father in heaven." (Whatever this clause means, it implies that the little ones should not be despised because their dignity is in God's eyes very great.) On the other hand, the shepherd, the Father Himself (18:14), is concerned for each sheep in His flock, so much so that He goes after the one that strays. After all, it is not His will that even one of these little ones, these humbled, true believers, should perish. If that is His attitude, it is an abomination for anyone else to try to make the little ones stumble.

But suppose that one of the little ones sins against another little one—against *you!* What are you to do? One of the remarkable things about Jesus' teaching in this regard is that despite all His emphasis on forgiveness and humility, He does *not* expect the sin to be swept under the carpet. At one level or another, it must be dealt with. And the level should quietly escalate.

Begin with personal discussion with the offender (18:15). If that proves ineffective, proceed in steps until the matter is brought before the church, the community of God's little ones, who may in the last resort take action to treat him or her as an outsider (18:17). This is a particular form of the discipline already introduced (18:18; see also 16:19). But in no case should the offender be let off while you, the offended party, seethe in suppressed bitterness. The offender must be encouraged, privately and if necessarily publicly, to turn from the offense; and the offended party must neither duck his or her responsibility nor retreat in wounded pride, but confront the offender.

It is in this context that Peter asked his unfortunate question about the number of times he should forgive an offending brother (18:21,22). To his brief answer, Jesus added a startling parable (18:23-35). The point was that the unforgiving servant had himself been forgiven a much greater amount. If the ten thousand talents were gold, it would be worth over a billion dollars in today's currency. Over against that staggering sum is the 100 denarii—about 100 days' wages for a common laborer, perhaps five thousand dollars. The purpose of the parable was not to suggest that we can earn the king's forgiveness by forgiving others, but to point out that all the forgiveness we are called upon to grant is a mere speck when compared with the grotesque amount for which we need forgiveness by the king. In short, the story powerfully responds to Peter's question.

If these patterns of behavior are adopted by those of us who claim to be disciples of Jesus, we will manifest fewer of the failures that stand out so pathetically and strikingly in these chapters.

Questions for Further Study

1. What do you think Matthew is telling us in 17:8?

2. What do Jesus' "how long" questions in 17:17 suggest about His own awareness of who He is?

3. How does the main point of 17:24-27 relate to the main point of 1 Corinthians 8? What relevance do these passages have for Christians today?

4. What sad scrambles for power sometimes take place among Messiah's people today (see Matt. 18:1,2)?

5. How does God view the sin of those who encourage or entice His "little ones" to sin? What relevance does this have to contemporary society? To the church?

6. Examine yourself carefully. Are you harboring any grudges against someone who has committed some offense against you, real or imagined? How, according to Matthew 18, should you deal with it?

In these two chapters, there is no startling new development, but a continuing polarization. There are two accounts of controversy—one between Jesus and the Pharisees (19:1-12) and the other between Jesus and His disciples (20:20-28). And all along, Matthew showed that Jesus' attitudes and values stood in marked contrast to those of the people around Him (19:13-15,16-30; 20:1-19,29-34). Out of the presentation of this controversy and contrast springs new teaching in several areas: divorce and remarriage (19:1-12), the sovereign grace of God in the dispensing of His benefits (20:1-16), and more.

Controversy

The *first* of the two controversial passages concerns divorce and remarriage. Few problems are so sensitive in many modern evangelical churches. Sad to say, by the time a marriage is heading for the divorce courts the entrenched bitterness, hatred, spite, and distrust are often so profound that there is an unwillingness to listen to what Scripture says at all.

Precisely because so many evangelical homes are breaking up, more and more studies of the New Testament's divorce pas-

sages are rolling off the presses. By no means are all these studies in agreement. The predominant tendency is to appeal to
some overarching Christian concept such as grace in order to
dilute the hard saying of Scripture on the subject. A few studies
err in the opposite direction and argue that the Scriptures as a
whole never allow for remarriage after any divorce.

A popular exposition such as this cannot possible canvass all
the options, or even offer a detailed defense of one of them.
Moreover, for a full statement on the matter it would be necessary to study many passages besides this one. Some help can be
found in major commentaries and studies. For the moment, I
shall simply sketch in what I take to be the shape of the controversy in this passage, and spell out a few obvious implications.

"Is it lawful for a man to divorce his wife for any and every
reason" (19:3)? That was the question put to Jesus by some
Pharisees. It reflected a theological debate common enough at
the time. One line of religious authorities would have given a
resounding yes to the question, going so far as to say that even if
a man found a prettier woman, that was grounds enough to
divorce his wife. The other main school of thought restricted the
legitimacy of divorce to cases where gross indecency had
occurred.

Both positions based their arguments in part on Deuteronomy 24:1, which allowed a husband to divorce his wife if he
found "something indecent" about her. The two schools of
thought in Jesus' day disputed just how far the term "something
indecent" could be pushed. In addition, some monastic groups of
Jews insisted that no divorce whatever was justified.

Certainly divorce was becoming an open scandal among
some Pharisees. Probably the divorced Pharisee best known to
us from this period is Josephus, the renowned Jewish historian.
Equally certain is the fact that the two principal groups, although
they disagreed over which divorces should be permitted, were
happy to accept each other's rulings in individual cases. In other
words, if the more lenient school sanctioned a divorce, the more
conservative school would recognize that divorce as legitimate
and sanction remarriage, even though the divorce in question
was outside their own rules. It was as if the religious leaders

closed ranks around their collective authority instead of standing up for the principles they espoused. And now Jesus was being invited to throw His weight behind one party or the other.

Jesus' answer to their question was in one sense delayed (until Matt. 19:9), because He was persuaded that their question was seriously deficient. It smacked a little too much of "What will God let us get away with in the matter of divorce and remarriage?" rather than "What does God desire for His creatures in this matter?" So Jesus delayed giving a direct answer and returned to first principles. He appealed to the Creator's purpose in the creation of the sexes: God made them "male and female" (Gen. 1:27) and said, *"For this reason* a man will leave his father and mother and be united to his wife, and they will become one flesh" (Gen. 2:24; Matt. 19:5, italics added).

The words "for this reason" in Genesis 2:24 refer to Adam's perception that the woman was bone of his bone and flesh of his flesh inasmuch as she had been made from him and for him. The man and the woman were in the deepest sense related. And *for this reason*—because the Creator made them so—marriages occur and each marriage is a reenactment of the one-flesh principle that stands as the very structure of humanity. A man and a woman who join together in marriage testify to this structure; "they are no longer two, but one" as God intended from the beginning. Thus their union is in a very deep sense *God's* doing and "what God has joined together, let man not separate" (Matt. 19:6).

In this light, divorce is not only unnatural—against the structure of humanity as God made it—but gross rebellion against God Himself. Jesus therefore sounded rather like the prophet Malachi, who not only referred to the book of Genesis (see Mal. 2:14,15) but quoted God as saying, "I hate divorce" (Mal. 2:16). Jesus had not yet directly addressed the question the Pharisees had raised; but He had overthrown the underlying attitudes behind that question and shown divorce to be the ugly, sinful, rebellious thing it is. Even if exceptional circumstances arise that *permit* divorce—about which I'll say more in a moment—it must always be remembered that *divorce cannot be achieved without sin, without falling into what God hates.*

But Jesus' opponents barely registered the point before they pressed on with what they judged to be the fatal weakness in Jesus' interpretation. If divorce is something God hates, then why did Moses, God's spokesman, "command that a man give his wife a certificate of divorce and send her away" (Matt. 19:7)?

Their reference was to Deuteronomy 24:1; and Jesus responded by telling them they hadn't really understood their own proof text. Moses did not there *command* that people get divorced, but regulated the divorces taking place by insisting that there be proper certificates of divorce and that the wife twice divorced must not return to the original partner (Deut. 24:1-4). Thus the most Moses did was *permit* divorce; and this permission was granted because he recognized that the human heart can be so hard, so sinful, that divorce becomes necessary.

"But it was not this way from the beginning," Jesus pointedly added (Matt. 19:8), saying again, in effect, that any treatment of divorce that simply argues about what may or may not be done is in danger of overlooking one basic fact: Divorce, even if permitted, is never a *good* thing, a God-ordained option for morally upright marriages, but a devastating sign of sin.

At this point, Jesus gave His own ruling: "I tell you that anyone who divorces his wife, except for marital unfaithfulness, and marries another woman commits adultery" (19:9). This is the verse on which considerable dispute centers. As I understand it, "marital unfaithfulness" is a larger category than adultery, and includes homosexuality and all other sexual indecency. What Jesus was saying, then, may be paraphrased as follows: "Anyone who divorces his wife and marries another woman commits adultery—though this principle does not hold in the case of marital unfaithfulness."

Strictly speaking, this ruling is both lighter and heavier than Old Testament prescriptions—lighter in that capital punishment is not here stipulated in the case of adultery and heavier in that the *only* exception is sexual sin of some sort. One can easily understand why sexual sin was treated as a special case, since the permanence of the marriage union is predicated in part on *sexual* union. Sexual promiscuity is therefore already a break. It may not *demand* divorce—there may be repentance, forgiveness, and reconciliation but divorce and remarriage are permitted as a *concession* in such cases.

There is, I think, one small extension of this exception in the writings of Paul (see 1 Cor. 7). Apart from that small extension, however, the burden of the New Testament evidence is this. Men and women should not get divorced, for that is hateful to God. If they do get divorced, they must not get remarried. An exception to this rule is made when the first marriage ends in divorce because of marital unfaithfulness.

The disciples found Jesus' teaching rather severe and cynically suggested that if He was right it would be better not to marry at all—as if the appeal of marriage is contingent on liberal divorce laws that will let you off the hook if things don't work out. Jesus responded that not everyone can live by this word—not *Jesus'* teaching, as the *New International Version* suggests, but this word *of the disciples*. In other words, not everyone *can* live in the state of continent celibacy that the disciples' cynical remark suggested, but only those who are gifted to do so—those born eunuchs, the impotent, those who have been made eunuchs (some court attendants were castrated as a condition of service in a position where they were surrounded by royal women; see Acts 8:26-39), and those able and willing to live as celibates for the sake of the Kingdom of God (Matt. 19:12).

Thus Jesus, like Paul after Him, commended celibacy for those to whom it is given. Far from backing down before the disciples' surly cynicism, Jesus said that for *such* people, they were right: "It is better not to marry" and "the one who can accept this [celibacy] should accept it" (19:11,12). But this does not mean celibacy is an intrinsically holier state (see 1 Tim. 4:1-3; Heb. 13:4), but a special gift to some people whose singleness has the potential to make them more useful servants of the Kingdom.

The *second* controversy took place between Jesus and the disciples (Matt. 20:20-28). It was precipitated by the approach of James and John, the sons of Zebedee, who asked for positions on Jesus' right and left hand when He comes into His kingdom. What they were after, of course, was a special share in His prestige and authority when His messianic kingdom is consummated—something they held to be very near, something they envisaged as taking place without any cross or any substantial delay.

As Jesus said (20:22), the disciples really didn't know what they were asking for. Naively, they sought power and glory, while they had no idea of Jesus' suffering to come. Still less did they understand that following Jesus might well involve real and prolonged suffering *for them,* or that the characteristic attitude of leaders among Messiah's people is service, not love of power and pomp.

Nevertheless, Jesus questioned them cautiously. Could they drink the "cup" He was going to drink? "We can," they confidently replied. "Cup" language in the Old Testament character-istically referred to judgment or retribution (see Ps. 75:8; Isa. 51:17,18; Jer. 25:15-28). Perhaps the brothers and their mother thought that the final conflict was about to take place; and during that conflict they imagined that though Jesus' side would suffer, sometimes lose, even face death—the victory itself was sure. After all, how could victory be denied the One who had already demonstrated He could raise the dead and control nature? So they were prepared, they believed, to suffer with Jesus on the short term. They could drink His cup.

In one sense, Jesus agreed with them: "You will indeed drink from my cup" (19:23). After all, James would shortly become the first apostolic martyr (see Acts 12:2), and his brother John would suffer exile (see Rev. 1:9). Even so, Jesus insisted it was not His role to determine who will sit on His right and left hand in the consummated kingdom. That prerogative belongs to the Father alone (Matt. 20:23). Here as elsewhere (Matt. 11:27; 24:36; 28:18), Jesus presupposed that His authority was *derived* from His Father, and His role was to be perfectly obedient to His Father's will.

There the matter might have rested, had not the other ten apostles heard of the attempt by the Zebedee family to secure the inside track. Their indignation (20:24) was prompted, one suspects, less by honest concern for fair play than by fear they might be outstripped by a clever political move they didn't think of first.

The ugly problem of 18:1-9 was recurring. And that was what prompted Jesus to call the Twelve together and teach the pattern of leadership that must prevail among Messiah's people. Ordinary patterns of authority in the pagan world must not operate here. Instead, "whoever wants to become great among you must be your servant, and whoever wants to be first must be your slave" (20:26,27).

Many of us have become so superficially familiar with such biblical teaching that we cannot easily feel the shock these words doubtless sparked when they were first uttered. Slaves could not rule; it would be almost as unthinkable if an untouchable in India were to tell a Brahmin to get out of the way. It is in the very nature of things that the high born and the ruler exercise authority, and the rest learn to obey. But in Jesus' kingdom, rank turns on service, leadership on self-sacrificing slavery to others. This is not so much a sign of weakness as of meekness, not so much a diminishing of authority as a humble way of discharging it.

And here, of course, the Christian has no greater model than Jesus the Messiah. If anyone *deserved* to be served, it was He; but when He came, it was not to be served, but to serve. This incredibly costly service extended all the way to His own sacrificial death. He came "to give his life as a ransom for many" (20:28). His life would go in exchange for theirs. As a slave could be ransomed by an appropriate payment, so the many are ransomed by Jesus' death in their place. Indeed there is probably a reference here to the last and greatest of the suffering servant songs (Isa. 52:13—53:12): "My righteous servant will justify many, and he will bear their iniquities. Therefore I will give him a portion among the great . . . . For he bore the sin of many" (53:11,12).

We can only imagine how immensely moving the memory of these words were to the apostles after they had seen the crucifixion of their Messiah and had time to compare their self-promotion with His own self-sacrifice.

Contrast
Even when the differences between Jesus and those around

Him were not so sharp as to erupt in controversy, in all that Matthew records at this stage of Jesus' ministry there is some kind of contrast drawn between Jesus and the religious leaders or between Jesus and His own disciples.

The *first* contrast lies between Jesus' attitude toward little children, and the attitude of His disciples (Matt. 19:13-15). Why they tried to prevent the children from coming to Jesus is unclear. Perhaps they thought they were being delayed in their journey to Jerusalem; perhaps they thought Jesus was busy enough already; or perhaps they thought children were negligible members of society who should not interrupt an important personage like the Messiah.

But whatever the disciples' motivation, Jesus would have none of their attitude. "Let the little children come to me," He commanded, "and do not hinder them." The reason He gave is of great importance: "For the kingdom of heaven belongs to such as these" (19:14). It is important to see that Jesus did *not* say the Kingdom of heaven belongs *to these,* but *to such as these*—not to children per se, but to those who are like them.

The thought is very similar to what we found in 18:1-9. So much popular religion encourages people to think that the pious person is the intrinsically superior person, the moral person is the one who enters the Kingdom, and the spiritually upright (who are often also spiritually uptight) are most popular with God. But Jesus insisted that the Kingdom belongs to those who approach Him from a position of spiritual bankruptcy (5:3). Not the haughty and self-seeking, but the humble and open—like children—inherit eternal life and find positions of eminence in the kingdom (18:1-9). The disciples' actions toward these children were therefore an acted parable suggesting exactly the *opposite* of what Jesus wanted to convey. He provided a warmhearted counter-example, and explained the importance of children as models of those who come to Him.

The next section (19:16-30) embraces a triple contrast. *First,* there is the contrast in values between the rich young man and Jesus. The former was prepared to go to considerable trouble to obey discreet laws if it would win him eternal life; but he was unwilling to deal with his divided heart. The young man sensed his spiritual dearth, and pursued Jesus with, "What do I still lack?" (v. 20).

Jesus replied that if he wanted to be perfect—if he really wanted undivided loyalty to God and full-hearted obedience—he would have to sell his possessions, disperse the proceeds among the poor, and follow Jesus. This injunction exposed the root problem: despite his moral pretensions, he had a divided heart. That divided loyalty is precisely what a true follower of Jesus *cannot* have. Obeying individual commandments cannot substitute for wholehearted, undivided allegiance and self-surrender to the Messiah.

This encounter provoked Jesus' reflection on the treachery of wealth: "I tell you the truth, it is hard for a rich man to enter the kingdom of heaven" (v. 23). More: "It is easier for a camel to go through the eye of a needle than for a rich man to enter the kingdom of God" (v. 24). It is flatly impossible! The disciples were astonished and asked, "Who then can be saved?" (v. 25).

It was the form of their question that betrayed the *second* contrast. Like many others in their day, they held that material prosperity was a divine blessing. Great wealth among the outwardly pious was a sign that an individual had won God's approval. So if *the rich* could not be saved, who then could be? If the wealthy were not approved by God, what evidence was there that He approves anyone?

Their question reflected far, far too much respect for wealth. Worse, it seemed to suggest that God's approval could be won, and even to some extent measured by counting up wealth. Jesus' assessment was radically different: far from being a sign that an individual is likely to inherit salvation, wealth makes salvation nearly impossible. And if this means that, so far as human ability goes, no one can be saved, then so be it. On this point Jesus agreed with His disciples and confirmed, "With man it is impossible." It is indeed impossible for men and women, by themselves, to be saved.

"But with God all things are possible" (v. 26). That represented *Jesus'* contrasting attitude. Hope for the salvation of any individual rests with God alone. As Paul would later put it, it turns on God's *grace*. Wealth that some treat as a measure of blessing drives people to the self-assurance and self-confidence that refuses to acknowledge the need for grace. Jesus' attitude was fundamentally different from that of His disciples on these points.

The *third* of the three contrasts in this section was precipitated by Peter (19:27-30), speaking for the Twelve. Apparently he thought Jesus' words a little severe in their case; for after all, they had abandoned everything in order to follow Jesus. Was there nothing in it for them?

In one sense, Jesus' reply was reassuring (v. 28). There was indeed something special for the apostles; they would sit on 12 thrones and judge the 12 tribes of Israel. But lest the apostles think Jesus was conceding that they deserved or earned this honor, He insisted that *everyone* who leaves anyone or anything of worth for His sake would be paid back "a hundred times as much"—and would inherit eternal life (v. 29). God is no one's debtor. If for the sake of following Jesus Christ we face total rejection by our own families, we discover that the people of God take us up and become a larger, stronger, tighter family than we have ever known.

The thought is very similar to 16:24-28. The person who seeks self-interest finds neither fulfillment nor eternal life. The person who disowns self-interest and cherishes Christ's interest discovers that even here God is a God of grace, repaying in countless ways and, in the end, granting eternal life. It is this sublime paradox that will generate the great reversal at the end: "Many who are first will be last, and many who are last will be first" (19:30).

What a contrast! Here was Peter asking in effect what he would receive in exchange for his sacrifices; and here was Jesus saying that although there would be a special role for Peter, he must understand that in the Kingdom God does not operate on the basis of exchange or merit, but on the basis of *grace*. The person who loses, say, a father for Christ's sake gains a hundred fathers—not to mention eternal life!

The next section (20:1-16) tells a parable to drive this lesson home, and thus continues the contrast between Jesus' approach to questions of reward and grace and that of those around Him.

The story proceeds simply enough until the various workmen start getting paid. Then the first workers, despite their agreement, feel slighted and cheated, and grumble against the landowner. The response of the landowner is worth quoting (and memorizing) in full: "Friend, I am not being unfair to you. Didn't you agree to work for a denarius [the normal wage for a day laborer]? Take your pay and go. I want to give the man who was hired last the same as I gave you. Don't I have the right to do what I want with my own money? Or are you envious because I am generous?" (20:13-15).

The point is that if God's generosity is to be represented by a man, that man must be different from any man we have ever met. God preserves a certain *sovereignty* when He dispenses His gifts. Those who think in terms of reward and merit can easily mistake God's gracious generosity for unfairness. What we need to learn is that God's abundance is *His*. In the world, the person who works hardest and longest should receive the most pay. That is just. But in God's kingdom, principles of merit and ability earn us only reprobation. They are all set aside so that sovereign grace may prevail. That grace generates the great reversal: some who are now first will be last, and vice versa (20:16; see also 19:30).

A *final* contrast is provided by the account of the healing of the two blind men (20:29-34). The crowds—willing to bask in Jesus' presence—reflected none of Jesus' compassion. They busily tried to silence the blind beggars who cried for help, while Jesus paused to meet their needs. It was almost like a crowd that tramples on a bruised cripple knocked down by thugs in its rush to get to hear a famous preacher expound the parable of the Good Samaritan.

The longer Jesus ministered, the more He stood out. Whether through sharp controversy or quietly drawn contrast, He stood alone in His mission, His attitudes, His grasp of the nature of the Kingdom, and His presentation of the freedom of grace.

Questions for Further Study

1. Summarize how God views divorce.

2. What practical steps can Christian leaders take to foster a servant mentality in their leadership? What steps can you take?

3. What does God owe you? Does God owe you anything?

4. What things besides money (19:22) give us a divided loyalty that keeps us from the Kingdom?

5. What are some of the ways God has abundantly made up for any "losses" you have incurred in following Christ (19:28,29)?

6. List some ways in which you may more closely practice the compassion of Christ portrayed in 20:29-34.

The Opposition Digs in—Jesus 10
Responds

Jealousy and hate often feed upon each other. If you start hating someone for some reason, the hate you feel very often distorts your perception of the individual so much that everything he or she does becomes loathsome and disgusting, utterly worthy of more hate. The very same actions perceived by another observer not consumed by hatred and jealousy might well be judged normal, friendly, eccentric, industrious, or whatever; but jealousy and hate fuel themselves by judging as malign everything to do with the hated object, and then by justifying the hatred on the basis of that perverse judgment.

The situation is sadder yet when the object of hatred is objectively good. That was certainly the case with the growing hatred and jealousy many felt toward Jesus. Their perverse judgment progressively distorted the evidence and fanned even more hatred into flame so that Jesus' very *goodness* became an offense to many. How grim, sinful, and pathetic the human heart must be if it generates envy and malice as its response to integrity, purity, and truth!

Jesus' Prominence and Integrity Attract Opposition

At this stage in His ministry, Jesus' opponents found everything He did repulsive or sinister. The first two scenes of Matthew 21 are not the sort that would prove to be exceptions!

In the first (21:1-11) Jesus was acclaimed by thousands of people as He approached the holy city, Jerusalem. The Roman military road from Jericho to Jerusalem passed near the village of Bethphage (a name which means "house of figs," reminding the reader of the many fig trees in the area and setting the stage for 21:18,19). The village stood on the southeastern slope of the Mount of Olives so Jesus' route would take Him over the mountain's brow and down the west slope.

That descent would afford Him a spectacular view of the city, rising to the heights of the next, slightly lower hill, the hill of Zion; but equally it would enable watchers in the city to detect His approach. So great was the enthusiasm for Jesus that crowds rushed out of the city to meet Him, joining the milling pilgrims that clogged the road all around Jesus (see John 12:12). The fever pitch of a great religious festival was raised even higher by Jesus' presence.

It is important to note that Jesus *arranged* for the colt He was to ride. This was not so as to manipulate the crowds—like a petty politician arranging for His own cheerleading. The praise would have erupted in any case. But the ride on a donkey, because it was planned by Jesus Himself, must signify something. In fact, it was an acted parable, a symbolic act of self-disclosure for those with eyes to see—or for those who, *after* Jesus' resurrection, would be able to fit the pieces together better than when they first saw the rather amazing sight.

What then did Jesus intend to get across by His action? Certainly the choice of a donkey was rather remarkable. Horses are often associated with war in the Old Testament but the donkey, a comparatively lowly beast of burden, was sometimes ridden by rulers *in times of peace* (see Judg. 5:10; 1 Kings 1:33; contrast Rev. 19:11). Moreover, Jews of Jesus' day understood that Zechariah 9:9 (quoted for us in Matt. 21:5) referred to Messiah, the promised king. So Jesus was gently signaling that He was fulfilling Scripture, that He was the promised king—but He did so with an act that had Him approaching in peace, gentleness, even docility, and not with the stern justice and vengeance many Jews expected the Messiah to manifest.

Judging by the crowds' fervent response, some of the symbolism, at least, was not lost on them. They acclaimed Jesus as "Son of David," the one who comes in the name of the Lord. So great was the commotion that the city buzzed with the question, "Who is this?"—a question which in this context was not asking for mere identification but for something more, some explanation. Some identified Him as "the prophet from Nazareth" (21:11). Did they hope as well that He was the prophet promised by Moses in Deuteronomy 18:15-18?

Crowds, of course, are notoriously fickle and in this instance such understanding as they showed was probably a mixture of enthusiastic hope, sloganeering, piety, and delight. But it was still unreflective, with no sign of profound understanding of Jesus' purpose and mission.

Jesus' next action recorded by Matthew is the cleansing of the Temple (Matt. 21:12,13). Because money paid to the Temple coffers had to be in Temple coinage, there was a considerable demand for the services of money changers. Moreover, pilgrims who came from afar much preferred to buy their sacrificial animals once they arrived in the city, rather than bring them from Rome or Ephesus or Alexandria. At the three great feasts each year, tens of thousands of Jews whose homes were outside Palestine flocked to Jerusalem, providing a market for those who sold animals. But what could have been a discreet service degenerated into a bazaar. The Temple areas resembled a market more than a house of prayer (see Isa. 56:7). So Jesus took decisive action.

There may have been another dimension to Jesus' rebuke. The words "den of robbers" are found in Jeremiah 7:11, which warns of the futility of superstitious reverence for the Temple, especially when that reverence is compounded with wickedness. Moreover, the word translated "robbers" more likely means "nationalist rebel" or "guerrilla." So Jesus was also charging that they had turned what should have been a "house of prayer" into a "nationalist stronghold" (to use the expression of C. K. Barrett). Questions of race and patriotism and tradition became more important than spirituality, prayer, and worship of the living God.

To this work of purifying the Temple, Jesus here displayed His miraculous healing power (Matt 21:14). While most Jewish authorities forbade any lame, blind, or deaf person from offering sacrifices in the Temple, Jesus faced a string of reversed decisions as He healed all who came to Him.

It was all too much for the chief priests and teachers of the law. It was precisely when they saw "the wonderful things he did" (21:15) and even the children praising Him that they could bear it no longer. Perhaps they were motivated in part by jealousy, in part by concern that the crowd reaction not become too exuberant lest it bring down the wrath of the Roman overlords, and in part by the embarrassment and financial loss His activity was provoking. Whatever the reason, they asked Jesus a question designed to shame Him into telling the children to keep quiet.

Jesus' answer was a masterstroke. He began by asking His own question—Have you never read?—suggesting the experts were more ignorant than they realized! The passage He cited is from Psalm 8:2: "From the lips of children and infants you have ordained praise." This is a marvelous response, for it simultaneously accomplishes three things.

First, it provides a biblical basis to justify Jesus' refusal to silence the children. This is something God Himself had ordained! Second and more important, Jesus was implicitly saying something very important about *Himself,* even if no one commented on that fact (so far as we know) at the time. The passage from Psalm 8:2 envisages praise directed *toward God;* but the children were directing their acclamation *to the Messiah,* the Son of David. Jesus' use of this Old Testament text to justify what the children were doing can only be explained *if He held that He should receive the praise given to God.* And third, the quotation reminds the reader once more that it is the humble—the children—who perceive spiritual truths and spiritual reality, while the sophisticated all too often spend their energies debunking or combating them (see also Matt. 18:1-5; 19:13-15).

Jesus' Predicts the Impending Division

We cannot probe all of the facets of the next section (21:18—22:14) very deeply; but even a casual reading of these paragraphs will convince us that the burden of Jesus' ministry at this point was to proclaim that the division taking place over Him was both expected and explicable.

The cursing of the fig tree (21:18-22) conveyed a number of lessons; but the one that concerns us here deals with Jesus' attitude toward religious hypocrisy. Fig trees sprout green figs (edible but not very agreeable) and then green leaves almost immediately after. So a fig tree in leaf normally advertises that it bears fruit. The figs themselves are not normally eaten until June; but a tree with a sheltered, southerly exposure might well advertise its wares a couple of months earlier.

Attracted by the leaves (see Mark 11:13), Jesus approached the tree, but found nothing but leaves (Matt. 20:19). Apparently this was one of the rare cases where the green figs had fallen off, unripened, leaving only foliage. If it had been the season for figs, of course, Jesus could have walked to the next tree and staunched His hunger there. But at this early period in the year, only the rare fig tree would have been in leaf—and this one was guilty of false advertising! Seizing the opportunity to make a telling point, Jesus cursed the tree—and it withered.

In addition to lessons about faith (21:21,22), it is hard not to see in this miracle a stern warning. The tree was not cursed simply because it was fruitless, still less because Jesus was having a temper tantrum. The point was that the tree by its leaves announced that it was bearing fruit, when in fact it was not. Jesus found nothing except leaves. The cursing of the tree became a model that pronounces judgment on religious hypocrites—people who make a show of piety but bear no genuine fruit of piety. The connection with the preceding verses is obvious; and the theme recurs again and again in this Gospel (see also 6:2,5,16; 7:5; 15:7; 22:18; and we are coming up to 23:1-39).

Still smarting, the chief priests and elders of the people demanded to know by what authority Jesus said and did all these things (21:23). Jesus responded with a question of His own, promising to answer if they would first answer Him: "John's baptism (his entire ministry, which focused on a public act of baptism)—where did it come from? Was it from heaven, or from men?" (21:25).

This was not cheap banter, a whining, "You play my game and I'll play yours!" Nor was it to suggest that if the rulers could not make up their minds about the Baptist, they certainly would not be able to make up their minds about Jesus. The challenge was much deeper, as the religious leaders instantly perceived.

If they replied, "From heaven," then Jesus would of course say, "Why didn't you believe him?"—and part of believing John was believing that John's witness about Jesus was true! In that case the religious leaders would have answered their own question. But if they said, "From men," they would run afoul of public opinion that held John the Baptist in high esteem as a prophet.

But in this case the authorities revealed the same moral bankruptcy displayed by Herod (14:5). If they decided questions of such great importance on the basis of what public opinion would allow them to get away with, they were unworthy to make decisions of this sort, and Jesus would not give them an answer. They raised the question of Jesus' authority; by His response, He raised the question of their moral and spiritual competence to judge such an issue. The divide between Jesus and the Jewish religious authorities was not only becoming clearer, but unbridgeable.

The three ensuing parables foreshadow the division that was coming. The point of the parable of the two sons (21:28-32) is that although the scum of society, the morally degenerate, begin by saying no to God, many ultimately repent, do what is bidden, and enter the Kingdom. By contrast, the religious authorities make a great show of saying yes to God, but do not do what He says, do not repent, and therefore do not enter the Kingdom (the words "ahead of you" in 21:31 are in my estimation a mistranslation and should be omitted).

The parable of the tenants (21:33-46) portrays a succession of evil judgments made by tenant farmers, until they go so far as to kill the owner's son. But it has often been God's will to exalt as leaders those whom others reject. That is the point of Psalm

118:22,23—quoted in Matthew 21:42. Whether the stone in the Psalm points to David—who was despised by Goliath, his own family, and even Samuel, yet who was one day appointed king by God—or to Israel—despised by the mightier surrounding nations yet chosen by God—is not important; for ultimately it is Jesus who recapitulated Israel as God's true son (see comments on 2:15 in chapter 1 of this book). And it is Jesus who was rejected as the rightful leader; but God would yet make Him the capstone.

This inevitably meant that the Jewish religious authorities and others who rejected Jesus' authority as the son of the "landowner" were the wicked tenants who would one day be crushed. The role the Jewish religious authorities played in mediating God's rule (His kingdom) to the people would be taken from them and given to others (21:43). The chief priests and Pharisees understood that the parable was about them (21:45).

Finally, in the parable of the wedding banquet (22:1-14), it is important to recognize that the king's invitation not only bestowed honor on the invited guests, but was tantamount to command. To turn it down was not merely rudeness, but rebellion. Adding injury to insult, those who were invited in this parable not only turned down the invitation but went so far as to mistreat and kill the king's messengers. Enraged by this assault on his honor, the king wiped the rebels out (22:6,7).

But the king's wish to assign honor to the son had to be satisfied; and so the wedding hall was filled with strangers rather than cancelling the feast. This did not mean these new guests had the right to come in some inappropriate fashion (22:11-13) but it meant that the great wedding banquet (a common symbol for the end of the age) would be celebrated not by the people who were most in line to enjoy it (the Jews, God's ancient covenant people) but by relative outsiders. Perhaps most shocking of all is that the introduction to the parable, tightly translated, means "The kingdom of heaven *has become like* a king who . . . . " The Kingdom *had already become* like the ensuing story. The invitations had already gone out, the fundamental rejections had already occurred, and the broader invitation had already been extended.

In short, Jesus anticipated and even foretold the divisions that would separate Him from many of His own people.

Jesus' Prophetic Wisdom Silences the Opposition

Even while the authorities were looking for a way to arrest Jesus (21:46), public clashes continued to be inevitable every time they confronted Him. Many in the crowds delighted in these impromptu debates, not least because most crowds side with the young challenger against established authority, so long as their own self-interest does not appear to be at stake. But the delighted astonishment of the crowds (22:22,33) did not mean they grasped the full importance of what was being said, or took it to heart for themselves.

The first debate was clearly a set-up designed to trap Jesus (22:15-22). It was the brainchild of an unholy alliance between the Pharisees, most of whom openly resented the Roman over-lord, and the Herodians, who accommodated themselves much better to the foreign power. Their question concerned the poll tax, the most obvious and fiscally painful sign of submission to Rome. Judea was a hotbed of nationalist intrigue, and many people wanted to throw off the foreign yoke. If Jesus answered yes to the question put to Him, He would lose an enormous amount of popular support. Indeed, in the eyes of many, a yes answer would have meant Jesus was *not* the Messiah, since it was widely believed that the Messiah would free the nation from the shackles of all foreign tyranny. On the other hand, if He replied with a firm no He could be reported to the Roman authorities as a traitor inciting the people to revolt—and that would be the end of Him.

But Jesus would not be pressed into an oversimplified either-or situation. He asked for a coin, the denarius used to pay the tax. As He held it up, everyone would know that on one side was a picture of the emperor's head, with the words (in Latin) "Tiberius Caesar, son of the divine Augustus"—offensive to any Jew who believed in only one divinity. On the other side were the words *pontifex maximus*—roughly, "high priest"—even though Jews believed the only true high priest stood in succession to Aaron. Jesus' question this time (22:20) could scarcely be ignored. The image was Caesar's, the inscription was Caesar's.

And then came the conclusion: "Give to Caesar what is Caesar's, and to God what is God's" (22:21). This was not simply a witty way to escape a predicament. Its true impact can be judged only when we remember that the nation of Israel was in theory a *theocratic state*—that is, God was seen as the head of the state, and the human king was His vice-regent. Thus if Israel was subdued by an enemy like Rome, it could only be because God was angry with Israel and punishing them.

This entire understanding turns on the fact that the people of God, Israel, constituted a state. Most pagan nations held somewhat similar views, modified of course to accommodate their polytheism. Religion and politics were thus bound together in the tightest possible way. But Jesus' statement envisaged a division of interests. He anticipated a messianic community, a church (16:18), *not* a state. Its members may have dual obligations: to the state and to God. But in principle, at least, the two are distinctive. Certainly Paul and Peter learned this lesson (see Rom. 13:1-7; 1 Pet. 2:13-17).

Elsewhere we learn that if the claims of God and the claims of the state clash, the former must take priority (see Acts 4:19; 5:29) but that the fundamental relation between Caesar and the people of God was changed by Jesus' saying there can be little doubt. Small wonder the people were amazed. They not only heard Jesus escape from a carefully set trap, but they sensed a staggering change in the relationship between Caesar and God.

It is not possible to take up Jesus' wisdom in responding to the Sadducees (Matt. 22:23-33) and the Pharisees (22:34-40), except to make one small point clear in the latter debate. Jesus in Matthew 22:34-40 did not set love *over against* law, but identified the greatest commandments *within* the law. All the law and the prophets "hang" on these two in the sense that nothing in Scripture can really make sense or be obeyed unless these two laws are obeyed. The old covenant, no less than the new, demanded a heart relationship with God (Deut. 10:12; 1 Sam. 15:22; Isa. 1:11-18; 43:22-24; Hosea 6:6; Amos 5:21-24). So Jesus' answer did not establish a legal requirement of the new covenant, but was a further denunciation of merely formal religion, no matter how orthodox, if it is not characterized by loving God and one's fellow man.

The final exchange (22:41-46) found Jesus going on the offensive. Until now He had answered His opponents' questions; here He turned the tables and asked them a tough one of His own: "What do you think about the Christ? Whose son is he?" At one level, His question was easy and the Pharisees' answer was right; the Christ (Messiah) is indeed the son of David. But if David in Psalm 110 wrote of the Messiah as "my Lord," then surely that simple answer was inadequate. After all, what *father* ever addresses his *son* as "my Lord"?

That was the problem Jesus set for them (Matt. 22:45,46), the problem that embarrassed them into silence. Jesus' disciples would come in time to understand the answer: although Messiah was indeed David's son, He was *more* than that. He was also *God's* son in a special sense and His birth into the human race as *David's* son was extraordinary. Another Pharisee would phrase it nicely once he had been converted a few years later. God's Son, he would write, "As to his human nature was a descendant of David"; but through the Spirit of holiness He "was declared with power to be the Son of God by his resurrection from the dead: Jesus Christ our Lord" (Rom. 1:3,4).

But if Jesus' opponents were silenced, they were neither persuaded nor disarmed; and so they were doubly dangerous.

Jesus' Pronouncements of Doom

That Jesus now denounced the religious leaders openly was not the result of snapped nerves, the final break of self-control. The situation was far more serious than that. The hypocrisy of most of the leaders was having a contaminating influence on the populace at large, and would sooner or later be exposed. If there was one sin common to all of the repulsive things Jesus cursed with His somber "woes" in Matthew 23 it was hypocrisy, religious humbug—especially punctilious concern for externals and statistics and appearances and prestige and honor; and very little grasp of the heart of Scripture, very little true worship, and even less concern for human beings.

But the woes were pronounced less in wrath than in tears;

for the pronouncements of doom end with Jesus weeping over the city (23:37-39; see also Luke 13:34,35; 19:41-44). No preacher is ready to preach judgment unless he waters his denunciation with tears. Jesus' pronouncements of doom were just and judicial. Yet far from being set forth with vicious glee, they cost the Saviour personal anguish and weeping.

Questions for Further Study
1. In what ways do North American Christians sometimes entangle the church in questionable financial practices and nationalist sentiment?

2. List all the ways final judgment is depicted in these three chapters.

3. Why did David address the Messiah as "my Lord"?

4. In what ways does the principle of 22:21 apply to Christians in North America today? To Christians in the Soviet Union? Should we try to set up a Christian state?

5. List modern parallels to the sins Jesus denounced in Matthew 23. How can we avoid them?

6. Can you think of other parallels in the Bible that link firm denunciation with profound compassion? Does this reflect something of God's character? To what extent should this combination be seen in our own lives?

The attempt to penetrate the future has always been a fasci-
nation to people. Some resort to spirit mediums, others to
astrology, still others to traditional but unsupported religious
interpretations—all of which the Scripture roundly condemns.
In our generation of readily available knowledge, there is an
entire industry built on predicting the future. Experts in this discipline usually proceed by analyzing the trends of the past few
years and then projecting them forward. Despite the immense
efforts that go into such work, however, predictions of this sort
are always predicated on the assumption that the present trends
will continue. If they do not, the predictions prove seriously
faulty.

Few topics generate more heat among some Christians than
eschatology—the doctrine of "last things," what the Bible says
will take place at the end. Central to this debate is the interpretation of Matthew 24 and 25, sometimes called "The Eschatological Discourse" or "The Olivet Discourse" because Jesus
spoke these words to His disciples on the Mount of Olives. This
is not the place for detailed discussion of various theories about
the end times. I shall simply outline the flow of thought in these

two chapters as I understand it. Those who want a more detailed defense of this view, and a fair bit of discussion of other approaches, can look at my much longer commentary on Matthew listed in the brief bibliography at the end of this book.

The previous chapter (Matt. 23) ends with Jesus' powerful prediction that the sins of Israel would be called to account in "this generation" (23:36). Jerusalem's house is about to be left "desolate" (23:38). Jesus would not be seen again by the populace at large until His glorious return, when the cry will go up, "Blessed is he who comes in the name of the Lord" (23:39). So it is not surprising, therefore, that the disciples linked the destruction of Jerusalem and the return of Jesus. When Jesus told them that not one stone would remain on another, so great would the sack of Jerusalem be (24:2) they replied, "Tell us, when will this happen, and what will be the sign of your coming and of the end of the age?" (24:3).

Birth Pains

Many Jews believed that immediately before the Messiah came their race would go through some terrible days. Some of them labeled this period "the birth pains of Messiah." Jesus picked up that terminology (24:8) as He talked about what must take place before His return.

Verses 4-28 can be divided into three parts. In the *first*, Jesus gave a general description of the birth pains (24:4-14). There will be wars, famines, earthquakes; nation will rise up against nation. Jesus' disciples will be persecuted, martyred, and generally detested. Apostasy will multiply, and be coupled with hatred and betrayal. False prophets will deceive many people and the increase in wickedness will cool the love and ardor of many others. The gospel of the Kingdom will nevertheless continue to be preached until it serves as a testimony to all nations and only then will the end come. Several important points emerge from these verses.

First, wars, rumors of wars, earthquakes, and the like do *not* tell us that the end is very near. "See to it that you are not alarmed. Such things must happen, but the end is still to come . . . . All these things are the beginning of birth pains" (24:6,8).

Second, although such things point to Jesus' return, they are characteristic of the *entire period* between His first and second comings. *Every single one* of these took place within the lifetime of the generation that first heard these words from Jesus and they have continued in every subsequent generation.

Third, Jesus' warnings presuppose that a substantial period of time will elapse before the end comes. It takes *time* for nation to rise against nation, and it takes *time* for the gospel to be preached in the whole world.

Finally, in any case, Jesus gave this outline not to encourage speculation but to warn His disciples against being deceived (24:4,5). Even social unrest will make the claims of false Christs seem plausible to the ill-informed. These false messiahs will dupe many precisely because the wars, catastrophes, and persecution will make them gullible, eager to accept instant solutions, panting to follow any leader who proposes a solution. But as Jesus' followers we are not to be taken in—a warning further elaborated in 24:22-28.

In the *second* part of Matthew 24:4-28, Jesus described one particularly sharp "birth pain," namely the fall of Jerusalem (24:15-21). Jesus predicted that the impending destruction (which would take place in A.D. 70) would be so terrible that those who would heed His warning should flee in haste. Many roofs were flat then; those escaping quickly might run from roof to roof and away, without even pausing to fetch possessions within the house (24:17). Those in the fields should not take the time to return to their homes (24:18). Flight is always harder in winter, and impeded on the Sabbath (which shows strict Jewish laws were still enforced at the time); and it is hardest on pregnant mothers and pregnant women (24:19,20).

In fact, Jesus viewed this destruction as the ultimate work of "the abomination that causes desolation." This expression was used four times by Daniel (8:13; 9:27; 11:31; 12:11) with reference to a number of destructions. But they point forward to this supreme sacrilege: "Let the reader [of Daniel] understand" (Matt. 24:15).

An historian who witnessed the destruction of Jerusalem and the desecration of the Temple after a siege of four years, described the horror. The famine was so severe that mothers ate their children. Rival groups within the city slaughtered one another and desecrated the Temple long before the Roman troops breached the walls of the city. The entire populace was either slaughtered or sold into slavery and the city was burned and razed to the ground.

There have been massacres of greater numbers in the sorry history of the race, but what destruction has been as cruel, so totally destructive, proportionately so ruinous as this? There have been more extensive judgments on the race—remember the Flood—but the fall of Jerusalem remains in a class by itself, if only because the distress was not only proportionately complete, but prolonged and ruthless. Indeed, that was Jesus' estimate: "For then there will be great distress, unequaled from the beginning of the world until now—and never to be equaled again" (24:21).

This is the sharpest of the birth pains of Messiah.

The *third* part of this section of Matthew (24:22-28) reverts to a consideration of the tribulation *throughout* the period between the comings of Jesus. Some have interpreted the words, "If those days had not been cut short, no one would survive" (24:22) as if they refer to the days of the destruction of Jerusalem. But there are very good reasons for thinking that "those days" refers to the *entire* period of distress. Here are but a few:

First, the word for distress is found not only in 24:15-21, but also in 24:9 (rendered "to be persecuted" in the *New International Version*). So when a few verses later in 24:29 we read about "the distress of those days," there is no reason why we must restrict the reference to the fall of Jerusalem. It makes better sense, as we shall see, to understand "the distress of those days" to be a reference to the "distress" first introduced in 24:4-14 as characteristic of the entire age.

Second, the words "*no one* would survive" (24:22) translates an expression that normally embraces *all humanity*. The verse would not be true if the reference were only to the destruction of Jerusalem.

Lastly, if the days are shortened for the sake of the *elect*

(24:22), we must ask who the "elect" are in the Gospel of Matthew. Wherever he used the term (22:14; 24:22,24,31; possibly 20:16), it refers to all of Messiah's people, all true believers, chosen by God. But if that is the meaning here, then the "distress of those days" cannot refer only to the fall of Jerusalem, since shortening the days of the siege of Jerusalem would save some *Jews* from death (though even so they were sold into slavery), but would not spare any of the *elect*—that is, Messiah's true disciples.

More important, these verses enlarge upon a theme introduced in 24:4,5, not in 24:15-21. That theme is a warning against being deceived by false Christs, false prophets, and miracles. When people become frightened, they are more easily duped by self-proclaimed heroes, religious leaders, saviours, and miracle workers.

Jesus said that all of this can be *expected;* and therefore we should not be fooled by it. Moreover, if any would-be leader claims to be Christ, or demands the devotion and obedience due only to Him, we must remember that when the *real* Christ returns, there will not be any doubt about who He is. His coming will be public, not confined to little groups of initiates—just as lightning in the east is seen in the west (24:27) and cannot be confined to a favored few observers. The enigmatic final proverb with which this section ends may simply mean that it is as impossible for humanity not to see the coming of the Son of Man as it is for vultures not to see carrion.

The burden of the first section of the Olivet Discourse, then, is that this entire age is to be characterized by distress, persecution, witness, opposition, wars, famines, and assorted false Christs whose purpose is to deceive God's people. This is far from the only passage that teaches such things. For instance, as far as persecution is concerned, Jesus elsewhere taught that His disciples should *expect* to be hated by the world (see John 15:18—16:4; Matt. 10:16-42).

Jesus was not saying that every Christian everywhere will face exactly the same opposition all other Christians face; but He *was* saying that distress, opposition, and persecution would be *characteristic*. Even a smattering of church history confirms much of this. There have alway been wars, rumors of wars, earthquakes, famines. And if believers in the West are *relatively* free of opposition, their brothers and sisters in Christ in China, Angola, Guatemala, Uganda, and Russia would be glad to remind them of what is *characteristic* of the age.

Jesus Comes Again

But distress does not have the last word. "Immediately after the distress of those days" (24:29)—immediately after the birth pangs of the Messiah—Messiah Himself will return. Amid cataclysmic celestial upheaval, the "*ensign* of the Son of Man" (for so the word "sign" in 24:30 should probably be translated) is unfurled in the heavens, and Jesus returns in splendor and glory to consummate the kingdom.

Sadly, however, this will not be a time of universal joy. True, the elect will be gathered "from the four winds" (24:31)—from everywhere, from all points of the compass—and they will be profoundly grateful and delighted. But "all the nations of the earth will mourn." When the Son of Man comes "on the clouds of the sky," which as in 17:5 symbolize God's presence, "with power and with great glory," many will be so terrified by His presence that they will cry for the rocks and mountains to fall on them and hide them from His wrath (see Rev. 6:15-17).

This, then, is the sketch of what Jesus gave to His disciples in answer to their dual question. The text will not answer our questions regarding the thousand years of Revelation 20 or other controversial subjects. But there is clearly still a sharp need to explain the *significance* of what the church must live through—the significance of the birth pains.

The Significance of the Birth Pains

Jesus explained that the relation between the birth pains of the Messiah and the coming of Messiah is like the relation between the sprouting twigs of a fig tree and the coming of summer: the one anticipates and heralds the arrival of the other. "All these things" (Matt. 24:33) cannot include the celestial signs and the coming of the Messiah, for then there would be no proper contrast between "when you see *all these things*" and "you know that *it is near*" (the coming of Messiah is near—or the phrase could be translated "you know that *He* is near").

It seems best to take "all these things" to refer to all the events in the distress-period of Matthew 24:4-28. In other words, in the light of His disciples' questions, Jesus sketched in the course of this age (24:4-28) and its climax in the coming of the Son of Man (24:29-31), and then turned to that aspect of His disciples' question that dealt with timing and connection.

Jesus made three points. *First,* "all these things" (24:4-28) must take place, and then Jesus' coming will be "near, right at the door" (24:33). In other words, the very next step beyond "these things" is Messiah's return.

Second, in that sense "all these things," all these distresses, point to that return—just as the fig leaves point to the return of summer, or yellow poplar and red maples leaves point to the return of winter.

And *third,* this generation will not pass away until "all these things" have happened. Despite various objections, the most natural way to understand the words "this generation" is to take them to refer to the generation then alive. For of course, what Jesus here predicted turned out to be strictly true: within forty or fifty years, all the things mentioned in 24:4-28 took place. There were wars and rumors of wars, devastating famines and earthquakes, serious persecution of the church and even martyrdom, the rise of false prophets and false messiahs, the fall of Jerusalem, the desecration of the Temple, and even the extension of the gospel to the far corners of the Empire and beyond. It must have seemed an incredibly bold prediction at the time; and perhaps that was why Jesus bolstered its believability with His solemn claim: "Heaven and earth will pass away, but my words will never pass away" (24:35).

Be Prepared!

Even though "all these things" took place within the first generation, it does not follow that they all ceased by the time the last member of that first generation passed away. They have gone on for many more generations. In any case, "No one knows about that day or hour [when the Son comes again], not even the angels in heaven, nor the Son, but only the Father" (24:36). So although the times of distress characterize the period between Christ's two advents, they do not in any way set up a timetable of the end.

Indeed, in one sense life has continued to go on. There have been wars and rumors of wars; there has been persecution and evangelism side by side; there have been assorted natural disasters. But the human race has continued. People still eat and drink, marry and give their children in marriage. There is nothing to suggest that the *final* cataclysm is at hand—any more than there was anything in human behavior to suggest the Flood was at hand in the days of Noah (24:37-39).

Or to change the scene a little, the coming of the Son of Man will be so unexpected and so sudden that it will find two men in a field and take one, leaving the other; or two women working opposite each other at a hand mill and take one, leaving the other (24:40,41). Whether the "taking" means "taken in judgment" or "taken to be with the Lord" is relatively immaterial; for the point is that the sudden cleavage testifies to the unexpectedness of the event.

After all, the coming of the Son of Man can be at an unknown time *only if* there is nothing terribly unexpected just before it. Disasters may be more severe, the persecution of believers worse, or whatever; but to most people these things will seem like more of the same. The hour remains unknown until it arrives; and then the cleavage is sudden, absolute, and irreversible.

The inevitable implication of this truth is that the church must always be prepared. It can never afford to sink into comfortable lethargy about the Lord's return, any more than it is justified in dissipating its energies in a frenzied search for the time of the Son's return when the Scriptures tell us that not even the Son knows the hour. So we must always be ready. It is that theme that occupies the rest of Christ's discourse in this section of Scripture.

Variations on Watchfulness
Although the parables in this section all stress watchfulness,

there are subtle and important variations in emphasis among them.

The *first* parable, about the homeowner and the thief (24:42-44), simply stresses the unexpectedness of the Lord's coming. In this one respect, the coming of the Son of Man is like the coming of a thief. This first parable therefore serves as a literary bridge connecting the following parables with the central theme established by 24:36-41. What Christians must learn individually, and what the church as a body must learn, is the importance of constant vigilance.

But this vigilance is not just passive; for in the *second* parable, about the two servants (24:45-51), there are duties to be discharged. The Master may stay away a long time (24:48—a subtle hint that the second advent might be considerably delayed) but when He comes, His judgments will be sure and final.

The followers of Jesus must always remember therefore that during the absence of their Master they are not only to wait but to conduct themselves as faithful and prudent servants—the more so, perhaps, if they are placed in positions of leadership over other servants. Whatever authority we as disciples of Christ possess we dare not forget that we serve Another, to whom we must one day give an account. Only that perspective will preserve some Christians leaders from claiming pomp and power for themselves, then degenerating into hirelings more interested in fleecing the sheep than in protecting them from ravaging wolves and leading them to good pasture.

The *third* parable, about the 10 virgins (25:1-13), teaches us that the delay may be longer than anyone anticipated, and therefore wisdom and foresight are necessary to prepare for the pressures of the delay.

The story of the 10 virgins meshes well with what we know of marriage customs in the ancient near east. If the groom did not live too far from the bride's home, he and some close friends would go to her home (usually the home of her father or brother) where various preliminary festivities and ceremonies would take place. Then there would be a procession through the streets, commonly after nightfall, to the home of the groom, where the main festivities would take place, often for many days. Guests and even the equivalent of some "bridesmaids" might wait along the way to the groom's house, intending to join the procession. Everyone in the procession was expected to carry his or her own torch. Those without a torch could safely be assumed to be party crashers or even brigands.

The plot therefore turns on the groom's delay (25:5). There is no moral blame attached to the sleeping; both the wise and the foolish virgins succumb to drowsiness. But the groom's delay distinguishes between the wise and the foolish virgins. The former prepare for the possibility of the groom's delay by bringing extra oil, and the latter are unprepared. Moreover, the preparedness of the wise can be neither transferred nor shared. "Therefore keep watch, because you do not know the day or hour" (25:13).

The *fourth* parable, about the talents (25:14-30), goes still further than the first three. The point of this story is that only those servants who make proportional *improvement* of the goods entrusted to them receive the master's blessing and reward when he returns "after a long time" (25:19). The dichotomy is so great that if a servant merely hangs on to what is entrusted to him he is considered not simply a poor servant but an unfaithful one, and is thrown "outside, into the darkness, where there will be weeping and gnashing of teeth" (25:30).

The reaction of the wicked servant is remarkable. He defends his action (25:24,25) by accusing his master of being hard and grasping, of exploiting the labor of others—"harvesting where you have not sown." So in a rather spiteful fashion he returns to his master what belongs to him, no more and no less.

But what the servant forgets is that in the logic of their relationships he *owes* his master his best service. He is obliged to discharge his responsibilities. Failure to do so betrays not only his lack of love for the master, but his own disobedient failure to live up to his responsibilities. His charges against the master therefore turn out to be a thinly-veiled excuse for his own moral indolence. Even on the servant's declared assessment, his actions do not make much sense, as his master points out (25:26,27). If the servant knew his master was so hard and grasping, why did he not put the money in a place where at least it would earn some interest?

In short, it is not enough for Jesus' followers simply to "hang in there" and wait for the end. They must see themselves for what they are—servants who owe it to their Master to improve what He entrusts to them. Failure to do so proves they cannot really be valued disciples at all. "The foolish virgins failed from thinking their part too easy; the wicked servant fails from thinking his too hard."[1]

Finally, the parable of the sheep and the goats (25:31-46) takes the variations on watchfulness one step further. These verses are rather unlike some of the other parables we have considered, in that there are no independent plot lines. The primary "parabolic" or metaphorical elements are the shepherd, the sheep, the goats, and the actual separation. But however we classify these verses, there is no denying their simplicity and power.

Nevertheless, the point of this parable (as I shall continue to call it) can easily be distorted. For instance, many understand "the least of these brothers of mine" (25:40,45) to refer to all who are hungry, needy, imprisoned, or poor. It follows that the basis of entrance into the kingdom is good works of gentle compassion, irrespective of belief, grace, faith, or anything else.

Certainly the ethical emphasis in this parable must not be diluted; but it is nevertheless essential to identify it a little more carefully. In particular, Jesus' "brothers" are surely His disciples (see also 12:48,49; 28:10). Therefore the fate of people is dependent on how they respond to Jesus' brothers—to Messiah's people, to Christians—as also in 10:40-42.

There is something more telling yet. The good works performed by the sheep or not performed by the goats, though clearly related to the ultimate destiny of each group, are not stated to be the *cause* of that destiny. Rather, such good works are the *evidence* of who these people really are.

This is proved by the fact that *both* groups are surprised by the verdict! Neither the sheep nor the goats are surprised at the place assigned them, but *at the reason the King gives for the assignation* (25:37-39,44). This means that how the sheep or the goats treated Jesus' brothers was not for the *purpose* of being accepted or rejected by the King—for then they would not have been surprised. The surprise of the sheep, for instance, forbids us from thinking that they acted this way *in order* to gain reward.

It follows that the parable is providing a test that eliminates hypocrisy. If this sort of conduct were simply a set of external criteria, then many of the goats would have been glad to make their hospital calls in order to pass the test. But in fact it is far more subtle. True disciples will pass an examination not because they are trying to pass an examination but because they *will* love His brothers and sisters—and therefore Jesus. Goats will fail because of course they *will not* particularly care for Jesus' brothers and sisters, and thus will be rejecting the Messiah Himself (10:40-42)—just as Saul, in persecuting Christians, was actually persecuting Jesus (see Acts 9:5).

Thus not only are Jesus' followers to await His return, but they must do so in a closely-knit fellowship. One's attitude to that fellowship of Messiah's brothers and sisters infallibly betrays whether one is a sheep or a goat, destined in the one case for eternal life, and in the other for eternal punishment.

Note
1. Henry Alford, *The Greek New Testament*, Vol. 1 (Chicago: Moody Press, 1958).

Questions for Further Study

1. What bearing does 1 John 3:2,3 have on the study of Matthew 24—25?

2. What bearing does the return of Christ have on your goals, values, hopes, fears?

3. In what ways does a Christian properly keep watch for the Lord's return?

4. What sort of conduct should the prospect of the Lord's return eliminate from, and conversely encourage in, Christian leaders according to 24:45-51?

5. How are you improving or multiplying, *for the Lord's sake,* the resources and gifts He has entrusted to you?

6. What will the King say to you (compare 25:34-36 and 25:41-43)? Why?

Few individuals leap from the pages of history with more profound irony attached to their lives than does the Lord Jesus Christ; and Matthew was aware of this fact. He noted that Jesus experienced hunger (4:2) but fed others (14:13-21; 15:29-39). Jesus grew weary (8:24) and gave rest to others (11:28). Although He was King Messiah, He paid tribute (17:24-27). He was called the devil but cast out demons (12:22-32). He died the death of a sinner but came to save His people from their sins (1:21). Sold for thirty pieces of silver (26:14-16), He gave His life a ransom for many (20:28). He who would not turn stones to bread for Himself (4:3,4) gave His own body as bread for the people (26:26).

But nowhere is this irony more pervasive than in Christ's death. His enemies believed they were destroying Him; but little did they understand that the destruction they achieved was God's means for redeeming a fallen world. Messiah's enemies thought that they inflicted the ultimate defeat; but in God's wise providence, that defeat was Messiah's greatest triumph. In the immortal words of S. W. Gandy:

He hell in hell laid low;
Made sin, He sin o'erthrew;
Bowed to the grave, destroyed it so,
And death, by dying, slew.[1]

Impending Doom

As I write this, the games of the twenty-third Olympiad in Los Angeles are taking place. After years of preparation, the event opens up with a solemn declaration—"Let the games begin!"

The first two verses of Matthew 26 function in that way. After centuries of preparation, after two or three years of personal ministry characterized by rising predictions about His suffering and death, after unveiling the sweep of the tribulation and hope to come, Jesus declared in effect, "Let the crucial step in the redemptive drama begin!" (See 26:1,2.)

All of the ensuing sections rush forward to make their contributions. The chief priests and the elders advanced their plot under the supervision of Caiaphas, the high priest (26:3-5). At first they determined to postpone their evil until after the Feast, when there would be less danger of public revulsion and rioting (26:5); but spurred on by the unexpected opportunity afforded by Judas Iscariot's offer to betray his Master (26:14-16), the plan was apparently updated, and preparations were made to put it into instant action when the right opportunity presented itself.

Meanwhile, in Matthew's topical ordering of events, he tells his readers of something that took place (probably a few days earlier) in Bethany (26:6-13). A woman, apparently Mary the sister of Martha and Lazarus (see also John 12:1-8), came and poured some "very expensive perfume" (Matt. 26:7) over Jesus. John 12:5 says it was worth about three hundred denarii—a year's wages for an ordinary laborer. Some considered this a waste (Matt. 26:8,9). Aware of their murmuring, Jesus rebuked them for bothering the woman (26:10). Then he justified her action on two grounds.

First, if anyone suggested the money would have been better spent on the poor, Jesus justified the extravagance on the grounds that He would not always be there, physically and in person, to receive it (26:11). Implicitly, of course, this was also a high claim; for His words meant that He not only foresaw His imminent departure, but that as the incarnate Son of God, the promised Messiah, He was *worthy* of this extravagant outpouring of love.

Second, Jesus related the woman's generous act to His own death (26:12). When a criminal was executed, the customary anointing of the corpse was often omitted. But this woman, whether she truly understood what she was doing or not, anticipated by her action Jesus' shameful death and burial. That connection would make this account live in the life of the church until the end of time (26:13).

The entire setting of the Last Supper (26:17-35) anticipated Jesus' death in many ways. For instance, that Jesus *arranged* the entire occasion (26:17-19) reminds us that He was no puppet, blindly forced to the cross by ill-tempered fate, but a *willing* victim, a *voluntary* sacrifice. The sad announcement of the betrayal (26:20-25) reminds us that, among other things, despite God's sovereign control of the entire cross-work of Christ, the guilty parties could not excuse themselves on that ground: it would still have been better for Judas if he had never been born (26:24).

And despite the protestations of loyalty by Peter and the rest of the disciples (26:31-35), they too would later abandon Jesus and leave Him alone in His hour of greatest need. But if that cowardice reflected their moral failure, it also reflected God's wisdom and planning; for Scripture foresaw this step (26:31; see also Zech. 13:7), a step that was necessary if Jesus was to be the sole sin-bearer.

Above all, this chapter gives us the words that institute what we today call "the Lord's Supper" or "the Eucharist" (Matt. 26:26-30). Jesus and His disciples were eating the Passover when Jesus "took bread"—probably a small loaf of unleavened bread. He broke it and said some words that departed radically from the customary declarations and responses at a Passover meal: "Take and eat; this is my body" (26:26).

Precisely because these words have no place in the Passover ritual, they must have produced a startling effect when they were first uttered; and they were foundational for generating a new remembrance rite for the people of God.

Both Jesus' words and His actions were pivotal. On the one hand, He broke the bread, and the body was to be broken; on the other, all must partake. It is doubtful if any of the disciples in that upstairs room fully appreciated what was going on; but by the time Jesus had risen from the dead, and they had grasped what His cross-work had achieved, they most likely brought their memories back to the scene again and again. And when they did so, they must have marveled at Jesus' clear-sighted willingness to face the cross, and remembered all the more fervently the *brokenness* of the body that won their redemption.

In the ordinary Passover meal, ritual demanded the drinking of several "cups." Probably the one mentioned in 26:27 was the third; but again, Jesus broke the pattern and introduced something new: "Drink from it, all of you," He said. "This is my blood of the covenant, which is poured out for many for the forgiveness of sins" (26:27,28).

The words "blood" and "covenant" come together only rarely in the Old Testament. Here the allusion was almost certainly to Exodus 24:8, where Moses ratified the covenant of Sinai by shedding blood. This could only have meant that Jesus understood the violent and sacrificial death He was about to undergo as the basis of the covenant He was inaugurating with His people. His sacrifice was modeled in part on the sacrifice Moses offered. Or, to put it a better way, the sacrifice Moses offered pointed forward to and therefore in a sense announced, anticipated, even prophesied Jesus' sacrifice.

There are still more connections with the Old Testament. If Jesus here announced the inauguration of a covenant, then it would have to be a "new" one—the "new covenant" prophesied by the prophet Jeremiah (see Jer. 31:31-34), a covenant in which God would forgive the sins of His people and write His laws on their hearts. The shedding of blood reminds us of the endless amounts of blood shed under the Old Testament sacrificial system—a dramatic presentation of the fact that sin can be paid for only by sacrificial death. Jesus' words "poured out for many" could not fail to be understood as a reference to the Passover sacrifice—but it would hint at other sacrifices too (see Lev. 1—7; 16), including the sacrifice of the suffering servant who "was pierced for our transgressions" and "crushed for our iniquities" (Isa. 53:5).

Just as the first Passover meal looked forward to a deliverance not yet accomplished, so the first "Lord's Supper" looked forward to a deliverance not yet accomplished. In the first case, the Exodus took place almost immediately, and entrance into the Promised Land decades later. In the second case, Jesus' death and resurrection took place almost immediately, while the final promise—a new heaven and a new earth—still awaits His return. Perhaps that is part of the reason why Jesus said, "I tell you, I will not drink of this fruit of the vine from now on until that day when I drink it anew with you in my Father's kingdom" (26:29). The Lord's Supper thus becomes a kind of veiled farewell and an anticipation of Jesus' return. Whenever the church gathers around this table, it not only looks back to the cross, it also looks forward to Jesus' return. This rite is only to be celebrated, to use Paul's words, "until he comes" (1 Cor. 11:26).

The Agony Begins

A very long book could be written about the verses before us; but perhaps it is just as well sometimes to skim more rapidly over the text and feel its total impact than to pause at every detail.

As the death of Jesus Christ was unique, so also were the agonizing events that led up to it. At the heart of this uniqueness is the fact that Jesus was not a martyr. A martyr believes so strongly in a principle or a cause opposed by the surrounding society that death becomes inevitable. In that sense, the martyr loses control of his or her own destiny. Not so with Jesus! A martyr could never say, "Do you think I cannot call on my Father, and he will at once put at my disposal more than twelve legions of angels?" (26:53). We must conclude that the Lord Jesus went to His death knowing full well that it was His Father's will that He should perish alone and abandoned as the sacrificial Passover lamb.

But though He was committed to His Father's will, Jesus

nevertheless faced the prospect of the cross with fear, loneliness, profound agony in His soul, tears. Up to this point, Jesus seemed to have exerted the sternest self-control in order to mask His anguish; but now, in an enclosed field on the side of Mount Olivet, in a garden called Gethsemane, He confessed to His most intimate disciples, "My soul is overwhelmed with sorrow to the point of death" (26:38). He meant His sorrow was so deep it was almost killing Him, not that He was so sorrowful He wished He were dead. Sadly, the three disciples who might have borne a tiny part of that sorrow for Him by watching in prayer with Him missed their opportunity and soon fell asleep (26:39-45). Jesus prayed on, prostrated by the profundity of His anguish.

The summary of His hour-long petition, repeated twice, betrays the heart of His struggle: "My Father, if it is possible, may this cup be taken from me. Yet not as I will, but as you will" (26:39). The "cup" here refers not only to His impending suffering and death, but, as often in the Old Testament *to God's wrath* (see Ps. 75:7,8; Isa. 51:22; Jer. 25:15,16; Ezek. 23:31-34). Jesus' agonizing prayer anticipated the rejection by His Father that He would sense most profoundly in Matthew 27:46.

In all of the various trials, beatings, and mockery Jesus underwent, His own character stood out more and more clearly against the backdrop of moral corruption, failed loyalty, and cheap cruelty around Him. Even the arrest was facilitated by a traitorous kiss (26:49). In days before photographs, newspapers, and televisions, many people would have only a hazy idea of what even a well-known figure like Jesus looked like; no doubt the authorities feared that in the gloom of the night Jesus might slip away or pass unnoticed in the confusion. And that is why an action designed to convey affection became an infamous symbol of love betrayed.

Even Peter's attempt to defend Jesus with a sword (26:51-54; Peter is named in John 18:10) was as pathetic as it was magnificent. His action represented magnificent courage. After hearing repeated warnings about the danger of defection, Peter felt the crucial test had arrived; and he resolved to prove he was as good as his word (26:35).

But his action was no less pathetic. Nothing revealed his complete failure to grasp the fundamental *reasons* for Jesus to go to the cross than his impetuous grab for his sword. He still believed that Messiah's kingdom would come with military might and spectacular displays of power against the Romans and against corrupt leaders. Worse, when he was rebuked, his moral courage evaporated so thoroughly that he fled like all the other disciples (26:56), and ended up cursing and blaspheming in a frenzied effort to distance himself from the Man to whom he had pledged undying loyalty (26:69-75). Physical courage he had aplenty; but when that proved useless, he knew no other kind. The most that can be said for him—and it is a great deal—is that when the rooster crowed he remembered Jesus' prediction, went out, and wept bitterly (26:34,75).

Judas fared far worse. He not only came to recognize that he was guilty of betrayal, but that the person betrayed was innocent (27:4). The money he returned ended up as the purchase price of a ceremonially polluted field where aliens to Israel's covenant could be buried; and there Judas did away with himself (27:5-10).

The conduct of the officials, Jewish and Roman alike, was no more attractive. Jesus confronted a Jewish court scrambling to find evidence, true or false, that would enable them to return a guilty verdict (26:59,60). Even Jesus' typological language about the "temple" of His "body" (see John 2:19-22) was used to suggest He was a hateful person who destroyed and desecrated holy places (26:60,61)—a serious charge in the ancient world.

Finally the high priest cut to the heart of the issue; he put Jesus under oath to tell whether or not He was the promised Messiah (26:63). Granted the commitments of the court, the outcome was now inevitable. Unable and unwilling to believe that Jesus was the Messiah, the court found Jesus' confession (26:64) nothing but blasphemy, blasphemy worthy of death. Unable to hide their venom any longer, Christ's accusers degenerated to searing mockery and uncontrolled thuggery (26:67,68).

Early in the morning, the entire Jewish supreme court, the Sanhedrin, came to a formal decision to seek the death penalty

(27:1,2), a sanction that could be granted only by the Roman overlord. A second trial was therefore necessary. In this trial before Pilate, however, the chief priests and elders of the Jews would have to cast their charges in political terms. Pilate would have cared little about messiahship, *unless* that messiahship entailed political authority that threatened Rome. The charge then became treason—a capital offense. Jesus was presented to Pilate as "the king of the Jews" (27:11).

Although Pilate was a weak and evil man, he was not a fool. He could see that the Jewish leaders, famous for their dislike of Rome, would not turn someone over to the Roman authorities if they honestly thought He could bring about deliverance from Rome. Their motives in this case therefore were suspect; and Pilate detected envy (27:18). But moral coward that he was, he turned Jesus over to them, and washed his hands to exonerate himself (27:24)—as if water could remove so deep a stain. Pilate could have let Him go (see Acts 3:13,14); but Pilate's political future depended on his ability to maintain peace, and fearing an uproar he decided his political future was far more important than the demands of justice.

The conduct of the governor's soldiers (27:27-31) showed humanity at its worst, the kind of conduct that breeds Auschwitz and torture chambers—the brutality of uncontrolled, unanswerable authority in a fallen world. The flogging (27:26) was standard procedure for prisoners about to be crucified; the savage mockery that followed (27:27-31) was not. The soldiers no doubt thought they were being deliciously ironic, hailing as king a man set to face the shame and pain of the cross. But the scene boasts far greater irony than they could have imagined; for Jesus was—and is—indeed the King Messiah to whom even these soldiers will one day give an account.

Crucifixion and Death

Two thousand years have elapsed since Jesus died on a cross; and pious believers everywhere have unwittingly domesticated what was once universally recognized as a savage and shameful instrument of torture. Today we wear gold crosses around our necks and in our buttonholes, we hang lighted crosses at the front of our sanctuaries, we print embossed crosses on our Bibles and hymnals. *And no one is shocked!* But all the ancient sources testify to how the cross was universally held in revulsion (see comments at the end of chapter 7 of this book). People who were crucified sometimes took days to die. Stretched out on the wooden frame, they would pull with their arms and push with their legs in order to keep their chest cavities open enough to breathe; and then excruciating muscle spasms would set in. They sagged, letting their bonds or their nails take the weight, until the need for oxygen started the abominable cycle again. Victims died of heart failure, of exhaustion, of shock. If the death had to be hastened for some reason, the soldiers needed only to break the victim's legs. Suffocation followed almost immediately.

But worse yet was the shame; and the shame was compounded in the Jewish world where everyone knew that the Old Testament pronounced the curse of God on all who hang on a tree (Deut. 21:22,23; see also Gal. 3:13). The gruesome sight drove the fainthearted and fearful away; the cruel came out to gloat over their success and hurl their insults and taunts: "You who are going to destroy the temple and build it in three days, save yourself! Come down from the cross, if you are the Son of God!" (27:39,40).

They thought they were so clever; but the foolishness of God is wiser than human wisdom. Precisely by voluntarily going to the cross, Jesus *was* destroying "this temple"—the temple of His body—and in three days it *would* be "rebuilt." And precisely because He *was* the Son of God, He would *not* come down from the cross!

Similar double irony extended to all the mockery He endured. "He saved others . . . but he can't save himself!" (27:42) they taunted. At one level, they were questioning the legitimacy and reality of His claims. Surely the *real* Messiah would not be forced to bear such shame and suffering. But at a deeper level, the taunt was largely right. If the Lord Jesus was to save others, He *had* to sacrifice Himself, and He *could not* save Himself.

But worst of all was Jesus' profound sense of being absolutely abandoned by God (27:46). This was not prompted by tawdry self-pity. The Son who knew the intimacy with His Father mirrored in Matthew 11:27 now experienced what He had never known before, and what He most dreaded—abandonment by His Holy Father, as He bore the curse of human guilt. Elizabeth Browning's poem is perhaps the best comment:

> Yea, once, Immanuel's orphaned cry His universe hath shaken—
> It went up single, echoless, "My God, I am forsaken!"
> It went up from the Holy's lips amidst His lost creation,
> That, of the lost, no son should use those words of desolation![2]

Triumph over Death—and a Commission

Thank God, the cross did not mark the end of the account!

By the best reckoning, Jesus was crucified on Friday. That evening, the Sabbath began (since Jews counted their days from sunset to sunset) and no one traveled very far. By Saturday evening, the Sabbath was over and the third day had begun. Very early on Sunday morning, at first light, two women, each named Mary, and some others (see Mark 16:1; Luke 24:10) "went to look at the tomb" (Matt 28:1).

How they hoped to get by the posted guard (if they knew about the guard before they arrived) we shall never know. A violent earthquake and the appearance of an angel terrified the posted sentries and they "became like dead men" (28:4)—they fainted in terror. What immediately becomes clear is that the rolling back of the stone, the appearance of the angel, and the effective removal of the soldiers were not to let the risen Messiah escape (as if stones and sentries could hold Him) but to let the first witnesses in.

None of the Gospel writers recounted all of the resurrection appearances of the Lord Jesus; but the various accounts can be harmonized in at least three different ways. We have reports of at least 10 or 11 specific appearances; and there were far more not recorded (see Acts 1:3). Modern readers cannot be eyewitnesses; but we receive by faith the report passed on by them and preserved for us in the pages of Holy Scripture. Not all the attempts to change or distort the truth—an example of which is found in Matthew 28:11-15—can remove this bedrock foundation of all genuine Christian faith.

But even the Resurrection was not the end of the story. In a sense, it was only the beginning. For Jesus, His triumph was the basis on which all of His Father's authority is vested in Him (28:18; see also 1 Cor. 15:20-28). This does not mean that before the cross His teaching and deeds were *less* authoritative, for even during His ministry His words, like God's, could not pass away (Matt. 24:35), and, like God, He forgave sin (9:6). Rather, the spheres in which His authority was exercised had now been enlarged. *"All* authority *in heaven and on earth"* belonged to Him, the entire universe under His sway.

Precisely because our sovereign Lord Jesus has all authority, His commission (28:18-20) is ensured of His power and the degree of success and triumph He bestows. The commission to make disciples, to baptize, and to teach them, not only remains one of the enduring mandates to the church, but brings together several central themes in this Gospel. Here is the fulfillment of promises to the Gentiles; here is the mandate to pass on all the teaching of Jesus that Matthew so carefully preserved; here is the fruit of the trainee mission recorded in Matthew 10; here is the authority or reign of Jesus already in operation; here is the forward-looking anticipation of the consummation to come ("at the end of the age," 28:20).

But the book ends, not with commission, but with promise (28:20). Our English "always" masks a Greek expression found only here, and meaning "the whole of every day." Jesus promises to be with His disciples, as they make disciples of others, not only on the long haul, but "the whole of every day," "to the very end of the age."

Note

1. Poem by S. W. Gandy in John Owen, *The Death of Death in the Death of Christ* (Edinburgh: Banner of Truth Trust, 1965).
2. Elizabeth Barrett Browning, "The Cowper's Grave" in *The Poetical Works of Elizabeth Barrett Browning* (London: Oxford University Press, 1951), p. 296.

Questions for Further Study

1. Did Jesus have to go to the cross? Meditate on 26:39,53,54.

2. Under what circumstances are you tempted to disown Jesus? What parallels can you draw with Peter's failure (26:69-75)? Do you, like Peter, end up weeping?

3. It is often easier to fight (26:51) than to pray (26:40-45). Why? What can you do about it in your own life?

4. Find all the places in Matthew 26—28 where Jesus' opponents spoke better than they knew—places where Matthew related the proceedings with profound irony.

5. How central to the Christian faith is Jesus' resurrection (read 1 Cor. 15:12-19)?

6. How do you help discharge the Great Commission?

A Brief Bibliography

(Inclusion of a book in the following list does not necessarily indicate agreement with the author at every point.)

J. A. Alexander. *The Gospel According to Matthew.* New York: Scribner, 1860.

Craig L. Blomberg. *Matthew.* In New American Commentary, vol. 22. Nashville: Broadman Press, 1992.

John Broadus. *Commentary on the Gospel of Matthew.* Valley Forge: American Baptist Publication Society, 1886.

D. A. Carson. "Matthew." In *Expositor's Bible Commentary,* vol. 8. Grand Rapids: Baker Book House, 1987.

_____. *The Sermon on the Mount.* Grand Rapids: Baker Book House, 1978.

_____. *When Jesus Confronts the World: An Exposition of Matthew 8-10.* Grand Rapids: Baker Book House, 1987.

R. T. France. *Matthew.* In Tyndale New Testament Commentary. Grand Rapids: Eerdmans, 1985.

William Hendrikson. *The Gospel of Matthew.* Grand Rapids: Baker Book House, 1978.

David Hill. *The Gospel of Matthew.* Grand Rapids: Eerdmans, 1972.

Alfred Plummer. *An Exegetical Commentary on the Gospel According to St. Matthew.* London: Robert Scott, 1915.

John R. W. Stott. *Christian Counter-culture.* Downers Grove: InterVarsity Press, 1978.